Pressure at work
A survival guide

Tanya Arroba
Kim James

McGRAW-HILL Book Company (UK) Limited

London · New York · St Louis · San Francisco · Auckland · Bogotá · Guatemala
Hamburg · Lisbon · Madrid · Mexico · Montreal · New Delhi · Panama
Paris · San Juan · São Paulo · Singapore · Sydney · Tokyo · Toronto

Published by
McGRAW-HILL Book Company (UK) Limited
MAIDENHEAD · BERKSHIRE · ENGLAND

British Library Cataloguing in Publication Data

Arroba, Tanya
  Pressure at work: a survival guide
  1. Executives — Job stress
  I. Title   II. James, Kim
  658.4'095   HD38.2

ISBN 0-07-084931-5

Library of Congress Cataloging-in-Publication Data

Arroba, Tanya
  Pressure at work.
  Bibliography: p.
  Includes index.
  1. Job stress.   2. Executives.   I. James, Kim.
  II. Title.

HF5548.85.A77   1987   658.4'095   87-3925
ISBN 0-07-084931-5

12345 AP   8987

Typeset by Barnes Design + Print Group, Maidenhead
Printed and bound in Great Britain by The Alden Press, Oxford

To Chris and Bernard

Contents

Acknowledgements

In this book we have drawn on the experiences managers have shared with us during our stress-management work; our thanks to all of them for their willingness to explore with us the problems they face. Our particular thanks go to Diane Merker whose hard work and dedication in typing our script has helped us greatly and reduced the stress of authorship. Thanks too to our colleague Kieron Walsh, whose constructive criticism of early drafts was greatly appreciated.

Introduction

1. This book and how to use it

Over the past few years we have become increasingly aware — both from our own personal experience and through talking to managers — of the toll pressure can take. In the 10 years we have spent working — as psychologists — on management development programmes the demand for special training in stress management has increased noticeably. One fact has struck us forcibly. While pressure is widely recognized as a part of modern-day organizational life, what to do about it when it gets out of hand is given relatively little attention. There are no magic solutions to the problems of inappropriate pressure and stress, but our aim in this book has been to put forward a sensible, if at times challenging, guide for survival. No one is immune to stress; our intention is to help managers work at a pressure level which is constructive and energizing, not destructive and draining.

Who is the book for?

This book is for managers, to enable them to develop strategies and skills for making pressure work in their favour, not against them. We all need pressure to function at our best, but pressures of the wrong type, or present in the wrong amount, result in stress. At a personal level, stress can mean discomfort, illness or early death. For the organization, stress means poor performers, inefficiencies and reduced effectiveness.

We believe that managing pressure in the context of the whole organization is important, but coping with pressure starts with oneself. If a manager develops a stress-related illness which takes him or her away from work or symptoms which impair performance, this will effect those who work with and for the manager. In addition, unless you demonstrate your own commitment to managing pressure and avoiding stress yourself, you will lack credibility in tackling the problems of pressure you see around you.

Whether you are just starting on your managerial career or nearing retirement age, whether you are working in a manufacturing company or a service industry, whether you are in the public or private sector, whether you are in a small organization or a multinational company, whether you are male or female, black or white, we believe that one thing all managers have in common is that both they and their staff work under a great deal of pressure.

What does the book contain?

This book is divided into two parts. Part 1 concentrates on managing the pressure you experience yourself and the steps you can take to ensure that you survive. This is your personal 'survival guide'. Part 2 focuses on the steps you can take to reduce stress in the organization. This is your organizational 'survival guide'. In each part we start by explaining how stress is created and how it can be recognized. We then explore the skills you need for dealing with pressure and reducing stress. Finally, we consider the strategies available for increasing resilience in the face of inappropriate pressure. Figure 1.1 depicts the structure of the book.

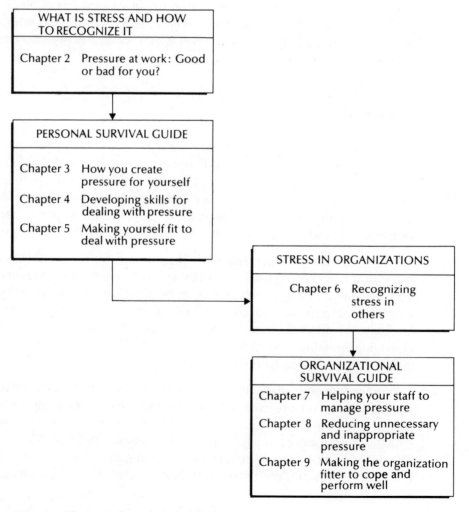

Figure 1.1 The route through the survival guide

How to use the book

Not every strategy outlined will be relevant to every manager reading this book. Only you can decide which elements are appropriate to you and your organization. We suggest, however, that you will gain more from the book if you read Part 1 first and focus on personal survival strategies before considering the organization.

We hope that reading this book will help you to think more constructively about managing pressure and to feel more confident in tackling stress problems. Getting the most out of the book, however, involves more than simply reading the ideas presented. At the end of each chapter are exercises designed to relate the ideas to your own experience and put them into practice. *Reading* through exercises will change little — you need to set aside time for *doing* them. Don't treat them as a chore, or this book could become yet another source of pressure! You do not have to get the exercises right or speed through them in a hurry; you need not stay up all night working through them; and you can do them with a colleague or friend if you wish. We hope you will enjoy this book as well as learn from it.

If any of the areas we cover particularly capture your interest we list some references to material we have found helpful at the end of the book.

Why read this book?

You will find this book useful if you identify with or are concerned about any of these:

- You believe pressure is a problem where you work.
- You frequently come home tense or with a headache, or feel excessively tired.
- Your staff frequently cite stress or a stress-related illness as a reason for absence.
- You think the atmosphere at work could be improved to make performance more productive and creative.
- You are concerned that your current lifestyle could result in early death.
- People at work seem unable to cope with the pressures they face.

When you have worked through the book you will be able to answer these key questions:

- Why does pressure need to be managed?
- What is stress?
- What causes it?
- What can be done to reduce or avoid it?

Your survival guide will:
- Help you and the organization become fitter to deal with pressure.
- Improve your skills for dealing with pressure and helping others cope.
- Provide ways of reducing unnecessary pressure by recognizing how it is created and maintained.

If an organization is to be successful, *all* its members need to be fit so they can contribute to the full. Organizations which rely on the survival of the fittest not only wreak havoc in people's lives but also fail to create a climate conducive to success. Managing pressure and reducing stress is not an optional extra for managers.

Part 1
The manager's guide to personal survival

In this part of the book we focus on you. As a manager you will face considerable pressure, and unless you manage it effectively you will eventually find that your performance is not as good as you know it can be, and you may succumb to the physical or emotional ravages of stress. Managing your own pressure level is an essential personal skill for you as a manager. You need to recognize how pressure affects you and design a personal survival guide.

In Chapter 2 we look at the relationship between pressure and stress and explore why stress is a problem. In Chapter 3 we look at the first element you can incorporate in your personal survival guide — recognizing how you create pressure for yourself and taking steps to avoid doing it. In Chapter 4 we add another element to your survival guide by outlining one of the most useful skills you can develop to deal with everyday pressure — the skill of assertiveness. Finally in Chapter 5 we look at the ways in which you can make yourself fitter to deal with pressure.

2. Pressure at work: Good or bad for you?

The manager needs pressure to be constructive not destructive. You need to make pressure work for you, not against you. You need to be able to perform under an appropriate level of pressure and not be stressed. To achieve this, it is important to understand how pressure results in stress, the factors that influence your response to pressure, and what causes an inappropriate level of pressure. You need to understand this in order to take a strategic view and ensure that pressure works for you. This will help you be more effective in your job and live a longer, healthier life.

Whether you are willing to take steps to manage pressure and avoid stress will depend on how you and the people around you view pressure and stress. Different organizations have different attitudes to stress.

Stress as a badge of office or a sign of weakness

The idea of stress as a badge of office is caricatured by the image of the 'two-ulcer executive'. Where this idea is prevalent, two ulcers, or some other symptom of stress, has the same sort of status as a larger company car. Suffering from too much pressure is seen as demonstrating to the world the high status of the manager. There is an assumption that as the level in the hierarchy increases, so should the pressure. If this is the case, the implicit argument runs, the manifestations of pressure should also increase.

In other organizations the pressures alone are seen as a badge of office, to be acclaimed openly, but any *symptoms* of stress are unacceptable. It is acceptable to complain of the pressure experienced, but to be seen to be having problems coping is taken as a sign of weakness.

This association of any manifestation of stress with personal failure is common, and places additional pressure on the individual manager to appear to cope, whatever the level of pressure and whatever the personal cost. People will then go to extreme lengths to cover up any symptoms, and a simple, friendly enquiry about an individual's well-being may be taken as a slur on personal competence.

The views you hold, and those which are prevalent amongst those around you, can influence your readiness to tackle stress as a problem. Stress can lead to illness, or even kill. To be effective and survive you must know how to manage pressure.

What are pressure and stress?

Pressure and stress are words which are often used interchangeably. They are not in fact the same. Everyone needs a certain amount of pressure. Pressure can lead to stress. No one needs stress.

Pressure is the aggregate of all the demands placed on you. These can be physical demands, such as those made on the body by jogging, flu, extreme noise, or getting used to different food when abroad. They can also be psychological demands, such as requests for your time and attention, dealing with difficult people, receiving a promotion or having too much work to do. Some demands are pleasant, others less so, but all add to the pressure you face.

Stress is your response to an inappropriate level of pressure. It is a response to pressure, not the pressure itself.

What happens to people under pressure?

We all have a level of pressure which is right for us. When pressure is not at this optimum level the result is stress. This will happen whether the pressure is too low or too high. Figure 2.1 illustrates this. The letters STRESS are used to symbolize experience at different pressure levels. Both high pressure and low pressure are inappropriate and thus stressful.

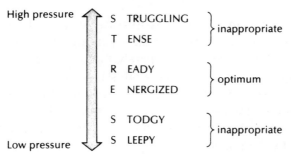

Figure 2.1 Responses to various levels of pressure: The STRESS continuum

The idea of a job where few demands are made of you may seem idyllic. When the pace is hectic and there is too much to fit into a day, daydreams of a silent phone, or empty diary and in-tray appeal. The occasional day of peace and quiet which allows you to catch up with a backlog can be enjoyable, but as a regular work pattern it is less satisfying. When the demands are few and pressure is low, most people respond by becoming less attentive and reducing their energy level — the 'stodgy' and 'sleepy' reactions at the lower end of the pressure scale. There is little point in being active when there is nothing to engage you. Far from being pleasurable, inadequate pressure brings boredom and stodginess. This is not the same as feeling relaxed. When work is not sufficiently stimulating there is little to look forward to, and little to provide satisfaction. Avoiding stress does not mean eliminating pressure, even if it could be done. To remove all pressure is stressful, as the experience of prisoners in solitary confinement shows. Clockwatching is tedious, as you will know if you have had a job with not enough to do or too much routine.

As the level of pressure increases, so does your level of alertness and attention. You respond by feeling and acting 'energized and ready'. This is the appropriate level of pressure for you, when you both perform and feel at your best. The optimum level differs for each person, and is not always possible to quantify (although we were told in all seriousness by one manager that an in-tray of two feet high was energizing, whereas at three feet, the tension crept in!).

As the pressure level continues to rise, feelings of tension increase and there is a sense of struggling to cope. When this happens, pressure is too high, and you experience the stress of too many demands. You may manage — by expending a lot of energy — to maintain a calm and unruffled exterior, but a great deal of tension and discomfort may still be experienced.

Moving marginally away from the optimum level of pressure will not present too many problems. Pressure slightly less than the optimum will be quite comfortable. Similarly, if the pressure rises only slightly, there can be a stage where the slight discomfort of raised pressure is an impetus to development and learning. It can be an important part of your growth and development as a manager.

It is at the extremes that pressure works against you. When pressure is either too high or too low, or swings between the two extremes, you perform less well, and therefore achieve less. Unfortunately the myth that a very high level of pressure is necessary to perform at your best is common. The idea that nothing is gained without a struggle influences many managers and often leads to a view that high pressure is the norm. This is not the case. When you are stressed you will not be working at your best. Even if you maintain your performance for a while, the cost will be high.

Why stress is a problem

Pressure works for you when there is a match between the demands you face and your capacity to cope effectively.

When demand does not match supply, as economists will tell you, the price fluctuates. With pressure, the price goes up, and unfortunately more and more managers are paying that price by attempting to operate in a situation where demand does not match supply.

In the short term stress is expensive, in the long term it can bankrupt you. The currency in which stress is transacted is *adaptive energy*. You have a store of adaptive energy, which is depleted by everyday wear and tear. When you are stressed, the rate at which you withdraw energy increases and you draw heavily on this store. Unfortunately you cannot manufacture adaptive energy; your supply is finite. Once you have used all your stock of it the body becomes unable to cope. Before the situation becomes fatal, however, your body will give you warning signals that you are using up your reserves of adaptive energy. To start with you might notice a headache or muscle tension; if you go on withdrawing energy you are likely to get a stronger signal that something is amiss. Your systems for adapting break down temporarily. The sign of this is often illness. Failure to respond to these signals and continuing at an inappropriate pressure level will result in early death. Between the headache and early death there are steps you can take to maintain balance. To do this you need information about the process underlying this drama.

How you respond to pressure: Your Stone Age constitution

Physiological processes have changed little during the very short history of 'civilization'. It has been said that we suffer from living in the space age with a Stone Age constitution. Modern offices and factories may be very different from the environments our ancestors inhabited, but our bodies are still programmed to cope with primitive and dangerous places.

Imagine you are back in the Stone Age. You step outside your cave and there charging up the valley towards you is a large, prehistoric beast. It is a large, shaggy mammoth, 14 feet high, with long tusks. What do you do? You have two main options. You can jump out of the way and run for safety, or you can stand your ground and fight. But above all, you need to react quickly; there is no time to deliberate.

This primitive ability to get yourself out of trouble is still part of our make-up today. It is known as the *fight or flight response* and it is part of your physiological programming. Pressure, in the form of threats to psychological well-being, has the same effect on your body today as mammoths did to our Stone Age ancestors.

Fight or flight today

The fight or flight response is amply in evidence in organizations. Let's look at two examples. If you are in the middle of a heated management-team meeting and a comment is made which threatens your position, you may well become aware of your heart beating faster. You may notice that your breathing speeds up. You may feel angry and clench your fists or jaw and glare at the speaker. But however tempted you may be to take a swing at the other person, you have learned that this is not appropriate. 'Civilized' people have learned to fight in less obvious, more socially acceptable ways. You may not take the swing, but you may deliver the sharp retort, striking with words instead of fists.

To take another example, imagine that your manager walks through the door unexpectedly and asks 'Who did this?', brandishing a report. You may come out in a cold sweat; you may feel anxious and want to run away. But you have learned not to turn tail and flee. You have other ways of defusing the situation, by removing yourself mentally rather than physically, by appeasing your mammoth or by ducking out of decisions.

In the first example we describe feelings of anger, and in the second anxiety or fear. They could equally well have been the other way round. Both are emotional labels attributed to the same physiological response of fight or flight. How you label the response and how you act depends on your perception of the event which acts as the trigger.

There are many sophisticated ways of fighting and fleeing at work. They have been necessary, or so it has seemed, to survive, just as they were for our ancestors. But are fighting and fleeing constructive responses to dealing with modern mammoths? The physiological arousal associated with the fight or flight response will not necessarily help you solve difficult managerial problems or deal effectively with others. Long-term damage can be done by repeated triggering of the fight or flight response. This becomes clearer when you understand what happens physiologically.

Fight or flight: The physiological reaction

Figure 2.2 shows the main elements of the very complex reaction which occurs whenever you perceive a mammoth or other threat. Your brain alerts your body to the need for action, triggering a chain of events starting in your central nervous system. This chain is designed to equip you with what you need for fight or flight. A virtual chemical orchestra of hormones is secreted. The endocrine system is one of the main ways in which messages are carried around the body, and when the hypothalamus alerts the pituitary gland at the base of the brain that a mammoth has been sighted, the chemical orchestra starts to play. The adrenal glands play the leading role and release more adrenalin into the bloodstream as well as substances known as corticoids. Both of these secretions play a vital part, not only in the short-term preparation for fight or flight, but also in some of the longer-term problems which can occur as a result of constantly fighting mammoths. The immune and inflammatory responses are inhibited while attention is on the imminent threat. The hormones act primarily to increase the level of arousal of your body. It is now on a war footing, alert to the threat and preparing to deal with it.

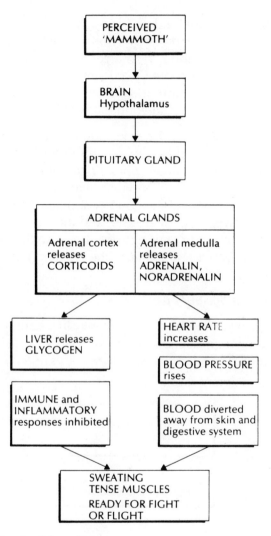

Figure 2.2 Preparation for fight or flight

Attention is then turned to the main transport system, the bloodstream. Not only does the bloodstream carry the chemical messengers, but it is also the main supply route for the fuel your muscles need. The most accessible warehouse for fuel is the liver, which releases its supply of glycogen. Your muscles need a greater supply of glucose so the heart rate increases and the blood pressure is raised. Whenever you become aware, in a tight spot, that your heart is racing, it is because your muscles are being fuelled for action. The blood is directed away from your extremities and your internal organs, and rushes to where your body thinks it is needed. In order to burn the glucose efficiently the supply of oxygen is increased, and your breathing rate becomes more rapid and intense.

While all the attention is focused on equipping your muscles for action, attention is taken away from your digestive system. Your body cannot cope with the normal processes of digestion and so digestion is slowed down. The final effect of the war footing is to activate the cooling system. You begin to sweat. Perspiration is designed to cool you down when you fight or flee, so that the body does not overheat when engaged in extreme physical action.

This whole reaction happens very quickly and effectively to prepare you to face a 'life or death' threat. If you encounter a modern-day mammoth and do not take the action for which you are physiologically preparing, the level of arousal will gradually fall back to its previous level. Unfortunately in modern organizations it is likely that you will encounter another mammoth before you have returned to the lower level of arousal, and the fight or flight reaction is again triggered. The problems occur not only because this reaction is being triggered inappropriately, but also because the reaction is prolonged.

How prolonged response to threat becomes dangerous

As Fig. 2.3 illustrates, when the body is constantly in a state of preparation for fight or flight, the short-term changes designed to get you out of danger can in themselves be harmful. The heart rate, which increases to get more blood to the

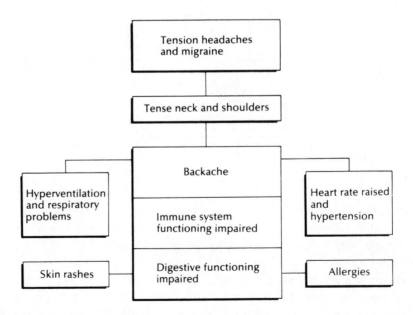

Figure 2.3 Some effects of prolonged preparation for fight or flight

muscles, can be permanently raised, resulting in hypertension ('high blood pressure'). This is one of the links in the chain between stress and heart disease. The rapid breathing which increases the supply of oxygen (needed to burn the glucose) can lead to hyperventilation and other respiratory problems. Prolonged release of the corticoids by the adrenal glands affects the ability of your immune system to respond. Cortisones act to inhibit inflammation and activate the defensive immune reactions and over a prolonged period make you less effective at reacting to invasion by foreign substances. This effect on the immune system is one of the links between stress and cancer. Muscle tension, so necessary for taking the swing or fleeing, maintained over a prolonged period leads to pain in the muscles, particularly in the neck, shoulders and back. The changes in the resistance of the surface of the skin due to sweating make it susceptible to rashes and skin disease.

You will not usually have problems in all these areas. Many people develop problems in one or two: bodies collapse at their weakest points. Where the weakest point is located depends on many factors. Two important ones are your inherited physiological traits and your lifestyle.

Stress patterns: Monitoring your response to pressure

Movement away from optimum pressure needs to be monitored. When people are under too much pressure they are often in so much of a rush that they fail to notice how stressed they are becoming. The earlier you notice that you are beginning to suffer from stress, the better positioned you are to take corrective action, before symptoms become severe.

Although the physiology of stress is common to everyone, you will have developed your own patterns of stress response. There is no definitive list of stress symptoms. Knowledge of the physiology can be used to guide your awareness of stress, but you need to identify your own unique response.

We are often asked by managers if their particular responses are 'normal'. There is no such thing as a normal response to pressure; there are only responses which are part of a regular pattern for an individual. A manager we met recently commented on having a numb nose when the pressure level increased. That is not 'normal' as not many people exhibit this response, but it was a common response for that person. The question of normality is only relevant in so far as it helps you recognize your own patterns.

To worry about things being 'wrong' or 'abnormal' is not a useful way of looking at stress. To put it neutrally, your system is giving you a message. When the pressure level becomes inappropriate you respond. That is the message you are getting via the raised heartbeat, clammy hands or whatever particular response you identify.

Looking for change

The pattern to look for when you are trying to identify your stress responses is the *pattern of changes* you experience when you are stressed. It is the change from your functioning at optimum pressure that is the key to monitoring stress. For example, some people are irritable all the time, others only when under too much pressure. Similarly, people have different resting heart rates, so taking your pulse is only helpful if you know what it is when you are not stressed.

As pressure increases, your whole system responds and any part of your system can show a reaction. The pattern will differ from person to person. For some people stress is manifested predominantly in one part of their system, but *stress can affect any area of your functioning.* There are four main areas of human functioning:

- Emotional (the world of feelings).
- Mental (the world of thought).
- Behavioural (the world of actions).
- Physiological (the world of physical responses).

Emotional responses

A change in feelings often accompanies changes in pressure level. Emotional change can be non-specific, such as a general feeling of depression or elation; or can be quite specific, such as a feeling of panic when certain things happen, or guilt about particular actions.

Mental responses

A change in your thought pattern often accompanies a change in pressure level. Some common reactions are finding it hard to set priorities, vacillation, procrastination, tunnel vision, and confused or illogical thinking. These are all very distressing in a job which demands rational thinking.

Behavioural responses

A change in your behaviour often accompanies a change in pressure level. There are many ways in which your behaviour can be affected. Common responses are an increase in behaviours such as abrupt speech, raised voice tone, irritability and generally hostile behaviour. A general increase in activity level is another common change; that is, more physical movement, more intense movement, more speech and faster speech, and more swings of voice tone. The opposite can also be identified — a behavioural clampdown or withdrawal. In this case the person responds to a change in pressure by becoming quieter, less voluble. Another possible reaction is a decrease in motor coordination, leading to increased clumsiness and perhaps even accidents.

Physiological responses

Physical changes often accompany a change in pressure level. Bouts of indigestion and headaches are physical responses often associated with stress. Muscular tension is another. Be careful not to explain such symptoms away in terms of draughts or uncomfortable chairs or beds. Of course not all physical changes are caused by pressure, but many are.

You need to be clear about the ways in which you tend to respond — do you feel differently, act differently, or think differently, or do your physical functions change? And in what way?

Sources of information for monitoring stress

It is very valuable to have people around you who are close enough to tell you about your behaviour. Close colleagues, secretarial staff and a supportive boss, for example, can all provide very useful information, but there needs to be closeness and trust between two people if such frank feedback is to be given.

Memory is another source of information about your patterns of response to pressure. You cannot rewrite the past to avoid stress, but you can learn from it. Remembering past reactions to stress will help you to become aware of your responses to various levels of pressure, so that you learn to read what your systems are telling you as they are telling you it.

The first three exercises at the end of this chapter will help you identify your stress pattern.

Attitudes to stress

Self-monitoring, however, is not straightforward. Your attitudes to stress, and those of the people around you, can interfere with your ability to pick up what your system is telling you.

Over the years, as we have talked to managers from many different types of organization, it has become clear that the images and attitudes associated with the term 'stress' are strong. These views can affect your willingness to monitor stress and your interpretation of what you notice. You need to be aware of any strong views you have so that they do not distort your ability to monitor change in any area of your functioning. Exercise 2.4 at the end of the chapter will help you reflect on this.

Stress: Reducing the high price of inappropriate pressure

Whenever you face modern-day mammoths you are exposing yourself to an increase in pressure. You need the ability to respond to threats to your well-being, but you do not need the fight or flight reaction to be triggered on a prolonged basis. If that does happen and you do nothing to restore the balance in your body, burn-out and exhaustion will follow. Exhaustion means physical or mental breakdown, and eventually death. If you do not monitor yourself for pressure, if you do not take account of the cost of facing modern-day mammoths, you will exhaust the supply of energy you have for dealing with pressure and pay the price. The supply of adaptive energy is one of your most precious resources. You make choices about how to spend this energy. If you use it by triggering the fight or flight response inappropriately, or subject yourself to prolonged periods of doing battle sitting in a chair, you will literally wear yourself out.

To survive pressure at work there are three steps you can take:
- You can re-evaluate your perception of 'modern-day mammoths'.
- You can enhance your skills for dealing with pressure.
- You can increase your fitness to cope.

These three elements comprise your personal survival guide. We will explore each aspect in the following chapters.

Before you go on to consider these aspects we suggest you explore your personal responses to pressure, using some (or all) of the exercises that follow. Exercises 2.1 and 2.2 focus on your recollection of events in the past to identify your patterns of response to different pressure levels. In Ex. 2.3 we suggest you monitor your current responses. Exercises 2.4 and 2.5 enable you to put together the information you have collected in the earlier exercises to give a clear picture of your personal response to pressure.

Exercises for Chapter 2: Understanding your response to pressure

Exercise 2.1 *Your response to pressure: What has happened in the past?*

By drawing on your past experience, this exercise will help you to identify your personal response to different pressure levels and become clearer about your responses when you move away from your optimum level.

Low pressure — Stodgy and sleepy

- Bring to mind a time when you were under *very little pressure* and when you were faced with few demands and challenges.
- Focus on what it felt like to be *you* at that time. Do not focus on the situation, but on your own experience.

– What can you recall *now* about yourself at that time? Write down your observations.

– Mark those aspects of yourself that you were aware of at the time and those you only recall now with the benefit of hindsight. You may need to pay particular attention to these latter elements, which will be more difficult to monitor.
– Can you recall any comments made to you by other people about your behaviour or appearance at the time?

Optimum pressure — Ready and energized

– Bring to mind a time when the *pressure level seemed right* for you and you were functioning at your best.
– Focus on what it felt like to be *you* at that time. Do not focus on the situation but on your own experience.
– What can you recall *now* about yourself at that time? Write it down.

– Mark those aspects of yourself that you were aware of at the time and those you only recall now with the benefit of hindsight.
– What comments did other people make about your behaviour at the time?

High pressure — Struggling and tense

– Bring to mind a time when you were experiencing *a high level of pressure* and demands being made on you.
– Focus on what it felt like to be *you* at that time. Do not focus on the situation but on your own experience.

- What can you recall *now* about your experience at that time? Write it down.

- Mark those aspects of yourself that you were aware of at the time and those you only recall now with the benefit of hindsight.
- What comments did other people make about your behaviour at the time?

Exercise 2.2 Your response to pressure: How does it affect you?

Think about your answers to Ex. 2.1. Focus now on the different parts of your system and how they changed in response to the different pressure levels you experienced. Write down your responses.

You may find it useful to repeat Exs. 2.1 and 2.2 using another set of situations, so that you have more data with which to build a picture of your particular patterns of response.

	Low pressure	Optimum pressure	High pressure
Emotional changes What emotions did you experience at the time?			
Mental changes How was your ability to think, concentrate, plan, decide, etc., affected?			
Behavioural changes How did you act? Were there any patterns of behaviour?			
Physiological changes What was happening in your body?			

Exercise 2.3 Pressure Diary

Using either your normal diary or a format you have specially devised, keep a record of your reactions to the various situations, people and events you encounter over the next few weeks, noting them each day.

Note your reactions in each area of functioning — emotional, mental, physical and behavioural — and see what patterns you become aware of as pressure levels change.

We suggest you keep this diary for two or three weeks to enable you to build up data from a number of different situations. This will help you become more aware of your reactions as they happen.

Exercise 2.4 How you view stress: A badge of office or sign of weakness?

It is important to reflect whether your views of pressure and stress could interfere with your willingness to manage pressure. Reflect on your responses to the previous exercises.

Badge of office

yes/no

1. Do you detect pride in your response to high pressure?
2. Do you view high pressure as desirable in your job?
3. Do you expect to be thought well of by colleagues if you are under a lot of pressure?
4. Would you expect people to approve of you if it became clear that the job was making heavy demands on you and taking its toll?
5. If you didn't feel under pressure, would you believe you were not doing enough?

Sign of weakness

yes/no

1. Do you take care to hide your responses to high pressure?
2. Do you think that any sign of stress could indicate that you have failed or lack ability?
3. Do you believe that competent people never suffer stress?
4. Do you feel ashamed or uncomfortable about 'succumbing to pressure'?
5. Would you expect others to criticize you if they knew that the pressure was high for you?

When you have answered these questions personally, go through again and ask yourself how the majority of people in your organization would answer these questions. If you have mainly 'yes' answers to either of these sections, then you need to re-evaluate your view of stress if you are to make full use of the information and exercises in subsequent chapters. If 'yes' answers would be prevalent throughout the organization you will have to work hard at the climate of opinion at work if organizational stress management is to be successful.

Exercise 2.5 Your stress response: What is it?

Drawing on all the information you have collected so far, identify your typical pattern of stress response.

When I'm under stress, _____

When I'm under stress, _____

When I'm under stress, _____

When I'm under stress, _____

When I'm under stress, _____

3. How you create pressure for yourself: Mammoths in the twentieth century

We all have modern-day mammoths in our lives. As a manager you will experience occasions when you react as your ancestors did when face to face with a real mammoth. Some people may appear 14 feet high and equipped with tusks; some tasks may seem fraught with danger or threatening in some way. Table 3.1 lists some common pressures faced by managers. While none of the situations poses a real life-or-death threat, each one can amount to a modern-day mammoth. It is possible, of course, to encounter physical danger in the modern world, even at work, and the fight or flight response is then essential to survival, but when the threats you face are threats to psychological rather than physical well-being, fight or flight is a less appropriate survival strategy, and a potentially harmful one.

The first element of your survival guide is assessment of the modern-day mammoths you face, followed by steps to bring the pressure level to a more manageable one. There are two ways in which you can manage the pressure created by your modern-day mammoths. The first is to arrange your life so that you do not encounter them. This, however, is rarely either feasible or practical. If, for example, a particular member of your staff has definite mammoth-like qualities in your eyes, it will rarely be possible to avoid that person altogether, nor would it be desirable.

- Management team meetings.
- Presentations to senior managers.
- Negotiations with trade unions.
- Interviews of any kind — selection, appraisal or disciplinary.
- Writing reports.
- Unpleasant working conditions.
- 'The boss'.
- Awkward customers or clients.
- Restructuring or reorganization.
- New legislation which affects the organization.
- Open-plan offices.
- New directors or managers ('the new broom').
- Informing staff about redundancy plans.

Table 3.1 Some common managerial pressures

The second, and, we suggest, more helpful way of managing the pressure of modern-day mammoths is to re-evaluate your reaction to those situations, events, people or tasks which appear threatening to you. You may be creating many of the modern-day mammoths yourself. How you react to what is happening around you depends on how you perceive it. The fight or flight response and the subsequent wear and tear on your body are set in motion by the brain. When the brain receives the message that a threat is approaching, it triggers the physiological process which leads to the pounding heart, dry mouth, shortness of breath, clammy hands or whatever your particular response happens to be. You create the pressure for yourself by the way in which you perceive events.

Perception is the process by which information is taken in through the senses and interpreted by the mind. It is the interpretation you place on the events happening around you which frequently causes a modern-day mammoth to appear. The common pressures listed in Table 3.1 appear harmless in themselves, yet for some people a mammoth is created because of their interpretation of the situation.

You may identify with some of the pressures listed in Table 3.1; alternatively you may be surprised at the situations which appear difficult to some people. What one person finds threatening will not necessarily threaten someone else. There is no definitive list of modern-day mammoths. Some situations, however, have a high probability of being seen as threatening, though the degree of perceived threat will vary. A selection interview, for example, is an event few people relish, yet it will not exert the same pressure on everyone. Public speaking is another example of something which worries many people but which others sail through quite calmly. The mammoths you face and the consequent pressures you experience are unique to you.

In order to re-evaluate your modern-day mammoths you need initially to be aware of what they are. You may find it useful at this point to turn to Ex. 3.1 at the end of the chapter and identify the aspects of your life which assume mammoth-like proportions for you. It is not enough, however, to be aware of what they are; it is also necessary to know why they are a threat to you.

We will focus in the rest of this chapter on the main ways in which you create pressure for yourself and what you can do to remove these manufactured mammoths by re-evaluating the situation. This means examining the main causes of threat to your confidence and equilibrium. Although the specific causes of threat will be unique to you, there are some general points one can make about why mammoths appear. They appear when you anticipate difficulties still to come, when memories of the past influence your perception of the present, when the things you learnt in the past no longer help you today, and when your basic needs are frustrated. These will be the main ways you create pressure for yourself.

Future threat: A problem today

You have the ability to conjure up pictures of the future. Your imagination is an important part of your defence system. By your ability to predict the consequences of events and actions you avoid a lot of problems. When the consequences are actually threatening or dangerous it is appropriate for you to be concerned and take evasive action. Even in this case, however, it is important that you do not exaggerate, or you will prolong the response to danger inappropriately.

We tend not to subject the predicted consequences of a threat to much scrutiny. How often do you stop to ask yourself: so what? You imagine all sorts of terrible things happening and once the fear, panic, anger or excitement begins, you forget to ask yourself whether it really matters. For example, if the consequences you dread are that you will not be liked, or that you will not be told that you have done well, or that your view is rejected, *it is difficult but still possible for you to consider these consequences objectively.* Would it be so awful for someone to disagree with you, or not to like you, or not to give you feedback? Quite often the consequences are far less dire than your imagination has led you to believe.

Some events can be perceived as threats because you fantasize about the kinds of things that will happen as a result. Your imaginings can be totally unrelated to objective information. You may predict that when a particular person takes over he or she is bound to ask for your resignation. You may think that saying no to a piece of work will lose you your job. You may worry that you will not get promoted if you disagree with somebody at a meeting. Each of these may be true in some circumstances, but, more often than not, these predicted consequences are quite improbable and a situation which could have been dealt with in a quite different and less stressful way is exacerbated by a sense of panic, fear or anger.

The key to whether or not the fight or flight response is triggered when you anticipate the future is the conversation you have with yourself. You rarely have this conversation aloud and at times can be unaware of it, but your inner dialogue tells you whether or not an event will be threatening. What goes on in your head may have little relevance to the real situation you face. A vital step down the route to survival is the skill of re-evaluating your internal dialogues so that they are based on present reality. This will lead to the fight or flight response being triggered less frequently.

Memories: How they create mammoths today

Imagine two of your Stone Age ancestors watching a herd of mammoths moving slowly across the horizon. At that distance the mammoths are harmless, but they do not necessarily appear that way to both people. For one of them the sight may recall a memory of being in the path of a charging mammoth. If the memory is strong, this person will probably perceive the herd to be closer and so more dangerous than it is in reality. What for some people will seem an ordinary, everyday, harmless event may to others appear fraught with danger.

The way you interpret an event today may be influenced by past experience. Particular memories can be recalled by something in the current event which is associated with the past, or the event may have a direct relationship with the past. For example, before my annual appraisal, I may recall last year's traumatic interview. It is not difficult to trace the links between the past and the present in this instance and once the link has been established, even if not consciously, I trigger the flight or fight response by telling myself that this interview is going to be as bad or worse than the previous one. I am by now probably feeling anxious or angry at the prospect.

More insidious, though, are the associations you make with events much further back in the past. The links are more difficult to become aware of because we only have hazy memories of our early years. Childhood experience is strong enough to influence our perceptions of events even in mature adulthood.

One senior manager identified management team meetings as triggering the fight or flight reaction because they were 'lively' meetings where people sometimes shouted a great deal. When this happened she felt extremely anxious and found it difficult to speak out and make her points. As a consequence she felt that she was looked down on as a junior member of the team. She said she felt rather like she had when she was young and her parents shouted at her. She associated raised voices with feelings of helplessness and anxiety. It was not surprising therefore that she found it difficult to contribute in a meeting where raised voices were commonplace. Most of us are sensitive to any sign of a recurrence of unpleasant experiences of the past.

Often the *feelings* associated with past events are carried over to the present. If the present has some feature which links you to a past experience, the memory of how you felt then may be incorporated in your present perception even if the feelings are inappropriate to the current situation.

To reduce the pressures caused by recalling the past you need to disentangle the past from the present. You may find it a useful break here to go back over your own list of modern-day mammoths. Can you trace a link between any of them and an unpleasant past memory?

Messages from the past: Do they help you today?

When you were young you needed to make sense of the world. Your parents and teachers in particular gave you guidance about how to behave, either directly by telling you how to do things and rewarding or punishing you accordingly, or indirectly by their behaviour. You observed how other people behaved and what happened to them. Gradually you made your own decisions about the nature of the world, which you translated into decisions about the way the world is and the way it should be. These form your core beliefs about how people do and should behave and think. You were probably not aware of making these early decisions but they were the conclusions you came to when making sense of your early world. Of course, we all reach further conclusions as an adult, but adults are usually more aware of forming new beliefs and values and how they inform behaviour. For example, from your early work experiences you will have formed beliefs about life in an organization. These will be based on what you were told and what you observed. From your thoughts and feelings during this time, you will have built up a complex picture of 'work', which will also have been influenced by your past experience of similar events — early school-days, for example — and what you were told about work earlier in your life. You will have made your own, unique set of decisions about the world of work which will continue to influence your behaviour until you re-evaluate them.

When you made decisions at those earlier stages of your life, you assimilated them as firm facts: that is how the world is and has to be. We are not always capable of recognizing that such impressions are only one way of perceiving the world. Those decisions were important for your survival: a child cannot go through life seeing only buzzing confusion. He or she needs to develop strategies for survival in a world where a child has little power and depends on others, just as a person starting work has to learn how to survive in the new environment.

To cope, children create their first survival guide. These are the strategies which seem to get their needs met most of the time. The world seems 'safer' if these strategies are followed. Decisions made in childhood have been part of you for so long that they seem immutable. You may not find it easy to question your own core beliefs, and yet you need to do this, to check whether they are appropriate for your life today. When you give yourself messages based on inappropriate or outdated beliefs suited to an earlier time of your life, you create considerable pressure for yourself.

One manager we spoke to recently identified a forthcoming promotion interview as a modern-day mammoth. He wanted the job very much, and although disappointment at not getting it would be quite understandable, his panic and extreme anxiety seemed rather inappropriate. As we talked he explained how he had not been as talented academically as the rest of his family and had always felt ashamed of being little better than average at school. He had formed a low opinion of his abilities and had made an early decision that his role in life was to be a good 'second-in-command', not a leader. He knew on the other hand that he was capable of doing the new job, but the tension produced by the conflict between his past decisions and his present assessment was intense. So, whilst an interview itself is demanding enough, his internal dialogue was placing even greater demands on him. He was experiencing panic long before he even knew when the interview was to be held. He needed to re-evaluate the issue of promotion by disentangling the past from the present.

It is helpful, when trying to tell whether past messages are influencing present actions, to listen to your internal conversations. An inner dialogue scattered with the words 'should', 'ought' and 'must' is a useful indicator that you are applying past guidelines to the present. You need to decide whether you still want to follow them and whether it is sensible for you to do so. The 'shoulds', 'oughts' and 'musts' are powerful messages. The manager who was anxious about applying for promotion found a number of examples of this kind of message in his inner dialogue: he thought he should try harder or get better (by applying for a promotion); he thought he must be content (with what he already had); he thought he ought not to put himself forward (even though he wanted the job). He needed to question these messages.

There are many inappropriate beliefs held about work and how to behave at work. At this point you may find it useful to turn to Ex. 3.2 at the end of the chapter and identify the messages you give yourself about work. By re-evaluating these core values you can save yourself considerable pressure and make appropriate decisions which are right for you *today.*

If you are unaccustomed to questioning these internal messages it is helpful to know that, even though everyone will have different experiences, there are some regular patterns to the messages people give themselves. These are common parts of the childhood survival guide. The messages you assimilated as a child were designed to make you acceptable and meet others' expectations. They became expectations you held of yourself, in a belief that everything would be all right if you behaved in accordance with them. There are five common patterns, or themes, to these messages; you may find that you use some, all or none of them. The problem is that none of them actually works in adulthood. They do not make you feel comfortable and acceptable to yourself and may not even satisfy anyone else's expectations of you.

Five common patterns of creating pressure

The five common patterns can be seen in various combinations; they are instructions you give yourself. They are extreme in that they are messages in your internal dialogue that include the belief that unless you do things according to the pattern, your well-being will somehow be threatened. They are extreme too in that you are endlessly exacting with yourself and no matter how much you try to follow the pattern you cannot do it well enough to be satisfied.

The first theme is the idea that whatever you do *you must do it really well.* This applies whether you are making children's building blocks into a tower, or planning a business project. However you do it, you must do it exactly right, and better than anybody else could.

The second is the message that it is the speed at which you do things that counts. It is good to do things very fast, so again whether it is building children's blocks into a tower or planning a project the essential element is that *you should do it really quickly,* so that you can get on to the next thing and get 'everything' done.

The third theme is the idea that it is the amount of effort you put into doing things that is really important. This internal guideline says that *you must try really hard* at doing this task. The key thing is that a tremendous amount of effort goes into it.

The fourth theme concerns doing the job single-handedly, even at personal cost to yourself. *You must do the job yourself.* Even if you don't know how to do it you should struggle alone rather than ask others for help or information.

The fifth theme concerns other people's approval. The message is that *you ought to do things in a way that will please other people.* The key thing is that you act in ways which suit other people rather than yourself. This means spending a lot of time guessing what people want so that you can please them.

Of course, individually there is nothing wrong with any of these expectations. There is nothing inherently wrong with doing things independently, putting in effort, doing things very well or very fast, or trying to please others. The problem arises when one of these messages overrides what is realistic and appropriate in a particular situation. These decisions or strategies are generated by you yourself but you may act as though they have the force of law behind them. It seems a matter of life or death that you behave in accordance with them — thus a modern-day mammoth is created. They are a source of unrealistic pressure because no one can comply totally with these internal demands, yet not to do so seems to threaten your sense of well-being.

These imperatives tell you what you ought, should or must do and often seem to be inscribed on tablets of stone. They are not. They are your internalized version of what you learned and decided years ago. Some were invaluable imperatives for you then. They may since have become obsolete. If you still act on them unquestioningly you need to review whether they are still helpful.

Frustration: Not getting what you want or need

Another source of pressure is frustration. If you do not get what you want or need at work you will create a mammoth for yourself. This frustration can occur in a number of ways:

- You do not decide what you want, so are never satisfied with what is available.
- What you want is not available; the environment is impoverished.
- You act in ways which reduce your chances of getting your wants and needs met.
- You have unrealistic expectations about how to get your needs met.

You need to evaluate whether the way you are behaving will get you what you want, and whether what you want is available in the organization; and, if not, you need to take steps to get it elsewhere. You also need to ask yourself whether your expectations about meeting your needs are realistic. First it is helpful to be clear about what you want.

If you were asked what you needed at work to make life better you might draw up a long list of items. You may want more resources, more time in the day, better equipment, longer tea-breaks, a salary increase, more interesting work or many other things. The combination of specific things you want or need to feel good instead of frustrated is personal to you, but underlying the specific items on the list is a set of universal needs which every person has. These needs are central to your well-being and when not met can lead to frustration and pressure. The first need we all have at work is for *recognition from and contact with other people;* the second is for *structure and stability;* and the third is for *variety and stimulation.*

The need for recognition and contact

Everyone needs a certain amount of contact with other people. To work in total isolation can be most distressing, as can an overload of people contact, which can lead to 'people poisoning'. Too much or too little contact can itself be a source of distress but it can cause additional pressure because it is through contact with others that the basic need for recognition is satisfied. Everyone has a fundamental need for recognition from others. At the very least you need others to recognize your presence. You also need others to acknowledge you as a person, who you are and what you have done. The extent to which other people approve of you, the degree of liking they have for you, and the rewards you get for what you do are very important to a sense of well-being.

It is very distressing to receive no recognition at all, to be ignored. If you have had the experience of completing a major piece of work only to receive no reaction at all you will appreciate this. Recognition and contact with others are crucial to psychological well-being and this applies at work as well as at home.

Recognition can be positive, when others like us or approve of our actions; or negative, when others show that they do not like us or are displeased with our work. We learn ways of getting recognition early in our lives. These can be related to the strategies we discussed in the last section. We may have got approval and positive recognition for doing things well, or doing things quickly, or getting a lot done. There are also other patterns of behaviour which earn recognition. For example, a family may give approval to one member for being amusing. We may carry the early learning about how to get recognition from others into the workplace — the family joker may become the office clown.

The decisions you make about getting recognition can cause confusion and create more pressure. Not everyone holds the same models as you do. If you expect recognition for perfect work, it may be a surprise to realize that others who are not as professionally perfect as you get promoted earlier. If your early learning was that recognition comes for being fast, it may be a surprise to find that people who take a long time over jobs are praised. If you have learned to get recognition for beavering away and getting on on your own, it may surprise you to find that others are rewarded for talking and chatting and supporting each other, which seems to you a waste of time.

Even in the face of a barrage of information which suggests that there are other ways of getting recognition from others, we tend to stick to the patterns we have learned because they feel familiar and comfortable. This will also be true if the recognition that we grew accustomed to when young was negative. If, for example, you are used to hearing comments about your mistakes or clumsiness, you will expect that kind of recognition. Because it is so painful to be ignored, negative recognition is better than nothing. If you have learned to expect only negative recognition you may, as an adult, continue to behave in ways which bring you negative rather than positive recognition. If you feel undervalued and unappreciated at work, this may explain why.

We perceive threat when our need for recognition and contact is not met — if we get no recognition or contact at all from those people whose opinions, judgement and respect we value, or if we do not get the kind of recognition we expect. There can be a mismatch between the recognition we receive and what we were expecting. We may have behaved according to our own set of rules, but that may not earn us any recognition at all, or not what we expected. If others do not respond as we expect, if they are not interested in us or if they seem to expect something else, we can become confused and suffer from increased pressure.

Let us look at an example. If as a child you were rewarded for being eager to please people, you will probably continue in the same way as a manager. If you are always guided by the desire to please, when your boss asks you to do more work you will very quickly be taking on more work than you can cope with. If your boss does not have a high regard for eager 'pleasers' you may not even get recognized for all the extra work you are doing. Your boss may soon appear as 'that awkward so-and-so' on your list of mammoths.

When you do not get enough positive recognition, or do not get it from the people you want it from and for what you want it for, mammoths will loom on the horizon. Two ways in which you can reduce the pressure of this unmet need are, first, to plan to get this need met elsewhere; and, second, to re-evaluate your expectations to see whether they are appropriate. Exercise 3.3 at the end of the chapter is designed to help you assess your expectations about recognition.

The need for structure and stability

We all need some structure and stability in our lives. We need some degree of predictability in the way we spend our time and who we spend it with. We also need some predictability in the kind of relationships that we have with people and the expectations that people have of us in our work. There are many things both at home and work which can disturb that sense of stability and structure in our lives, and these can be powerful threats even before they actually happen. You may only know that change is on the horizon, but that can be enough to constitute a modern-day mammoth.

How can change be threatening? For some people changing from one office to another may be an overwhelming difficulty. For other people the changes which threaten their structure and stability will be events such as a takeover or restructuring of the organization, or the appointment of a director with a brief to make dramatic improvements. This kind of event can disrupt your expectations about how you are going to spend time. How you spend your time will determine, to a large extent, the kind of contact that you have with other people and the amount of recognition you receive. Anything which seems likely to disturb your pattern of contacts with others can appear to be threatening. Change can also alter what you do. The expectations that people have of you in your role may become uncertain, and you may not be sure that you will be able to do the new job. Change can also alter your relationships at work; not just who you have contact with, but the nature of the relationships. With promotion, somebody who was a colleague last week may report to you this week, and this alters the structure of your relationships. When a major organizational change is on the horizon you may fear that your services will no longer be required — the ultimate form of negative recognition at work.

When you go through a change there are not only the direct problems to be solved of coming to grips with new structures, learning a new job or new technology, understanding a new manager's point of view or working within a new framework. You also undergo the process of saying goodbye to the old, before being able to welcome the new, and this will cause a 'wobble' in your psychological well-being. During that period of 'wobble' — whether it lasts half an hour, for a small change, or several months or years, for really major changes in your life — it will be quite common to run through a whole range of emotions as the mammoth on the horizon starts to charge. Exercise 3.4 at the end of the chapter will help you to assess the ways in which your need for structure and stability is met.

The need for variety and stimulation

Another need we all have is for a certain level of variety and stimulation. When the level is too low or too high we feel threatened.

Most managers expect to be stimulated and have variety at work, whether it is from the use of professional skills, from managing people, or from solving problems. All of these are appropriate and safe ways of getting stimulation which are helpful to the organization.

There are other ways of getting variety and stimulation which are less safe for the individual and the organization. A common one is the setting or acceptance of deadlines which are far too short. You then have to energize all your staff and your own resources to meet the deadline. This causes a flurry of excitement, in which people are spurred on by uncertainty about whether the deadline will be met. This is not a very safe way of getting the variety, challenge and stimulation which are needed. It involves a great deal of emotional energy, which may be stimulating, but the wear and tear on your body is helpful neither to you nor to the organization in the long term.

The need for stimulation also affects what you do outside work. For example, many people drive fast and dangerously to satisfy the need for excitement. By such activities you may be raising your level of stimulation but you may increase your pressure level too far. Being optimally under pressure is a very pleasant feeling. The problem arises when you provide yourself with the pressure in a way which is dangerous rather than simply stimulating. Driving fast is not the only dangerous way. Many things we agree to undertake at work can also be dangerous to health and well-being. Creating threats or things to worry about to increase stimulation often leads to struggle and tenseness rather than simply a state of being ready and energized. It may be helpful to look at other ways of creating excitement, variety, stimulation and challenge safely at work. You may also need to look at your whole life to see whether you are getting enough variety and excitement; and this may involve making sure that you are getting enough comfort, care and recognition. Getting excitement in a dangerous way can sometimes be compensation for lack of these.

You may find it useful to turn to Ex. 3.5 at the end of the chapter which is designed to help you assess where you get your variety and stimulation and whether it is a sensible pattern.

Everyone needs recognition and contact with others, structure and stability, and variety and stimulation at work. They are universal needs. You can, however, create pressure for yourself when these needs are not met, or are met inappropriately. The pressure that we have talked about in this chapter is of your own creation. You need to re-evaluate your past experience so that survival strategies you created for different situations are not inappropriately applied to current events. You need to see things clearly; you need to get your needs met skilfully; you need to avoid 'catastrophizing' about the future. These are the first ingredients of your survival guide for managing pressure.

We suggest that you take some time to assess your own mammoths, how you create the pressure for yourself and how you can re-evaluate the pressures, by turning to Ex. 3.6. When you have removed some of the mammoths you face by re-evaluating them, the next chapter looks at the skills you can use for dealing with the mammoths that remain.

Exercises for Chapter 3: Understanding how you create pressure for yourself

Exercise 3.1 What are your modern-day mammoths?

In this exercise we ask you to identify your modern-day mammoths. This is important because you need to identify the major sources of pressure facing you in order to plan ways of dealing effectively with them.

Focus on those aspects of your life where there is too much pressure for you. Think of the situations where the fight or flight reaction is triggered. Think too of the more insidious pressures which build up over time. Your mammoths may be *situations* where there is pressure, *people* with whom dealings are stressful or *tasks* which put pressure on you.

What are your modern-day mammoths?

Exercise 3.2 What are your old decisions about work? Are they appropriate now?

The purpose of this exercise is see how you put extra demands on yourself by the expectations you have.

Over the next few days be alert to the messages you give yourself about work. Some of the words you use give clues that you are using old decisions, in particular the words 'should', 'ought' and 'must' and judgemental phrases, particularly generalizations. Be aware of what you say to other people as well as your inner dialogue. Then write down as many of the messages as you can, in the form of the following sentences:

1. Work should be

2. At work I (and others) ought to

3. To be OK at work I must

Now go through these to ask yourself whether these beliefs are always true. This will not be easy if they are firmly held because you will have little experience of questioning them. Ask yourself whether you always want to behave according to these old beliefs. As an adult you have choice about whether you comply with them or not.

Try repeating each message to yourself and then stating the converse. For example:

1.   Work should be a struggle. Work need not be a struggle. I can make work a struggle *if I choose to.*
2.   At work I ought to make every effort to get things right. At work I need not make every effort to get things right. I can do so and *I have the choice.*
3.   To be OK at work I must know how to do everything in my job. To be OK at work I must not know how to do everything in my job. I can learn and *I have the choice.*

Be aware of the choices you have. Next time you hear a 'should', 'ought' or 'must' in your internal dialogue stop and say:

- Is this true?
- Do I want to do this?
- What other views are there?

Make new decisions where these can help you reduce your internal sources of pressure.

Exercise 3.3 Frustration and getting what you want: Recognition and contact

Are your expectations about recognition appropriate? Start by identifying your early experience of recognition.

What kind of things do you remember getting attention and recognition for when you were young? Was it positive (praise, smiles, etc.) or negative (rebukes, frowns, etc.)? Mark those which were familiar and frequent.

Positive   Negative

Mainly for being me — nothing in particular!
For doing well at school or sports (or other 'work')
For being willing to have a go and being persistent
For being strong and independent, not relying on
    others
For being funny and making people laugh
For getting things done quickly
For not making a fuss about problems
For being considerate and caring for others first
For trying something difficult
For succeeding, coming top or first
For joining clubs and teams, being part of a group
For being a leader
For being busy and industrious
For playing stupid or clumsy
For always being helpful
For being quiet and unobtrusive
For being loud and demanding
For being average at school or sports (or other
    'work')
For doing my best even if this wasn't good
For being messy
For being fun and not serious
For saying 'yes' when told to do something
For asking 'why?'
For grabbing new opportunities
For ....
For ....
For ....

All, some or none of these will apply to you — add in as many of your own as you wish.
Now look at your pattern.

- It is largely positive or negative, or is it mixed?
- Are any of the aspects given recognition in your childhood still important to you now?
- Are any of those that are important to you missing from your work life?
- Which others would you like to get recognition for at work? Do you get that recognition at work?

- Do any elements of your work — job description, profession, organization, manager, colleagues — conflict with the possibility of getting the kind of recognition you would like and feel comfortable with?
- Do you get recognition at work for any things which you didn't mark here? *Do you 'accept and hear' that recognition, or does it seem too unfamiliar?* (Perhaps you have never thought of it as recognition.)

Exercise 3.4 *Frustration and getting what you want: Structure and stability*

How do you spend your time at work? Imagine a continuum from 'on your own' through to 'intimate talk with someone else':

On your own (writing, thinking, looking out of the windows)	→Little rituals (Hello, how are you? — Fine, thanks)	→Chatting (about the weather, the government)	→Doing work together (projects, team meetings, committees, appraisals)	→Intimate conver- sation (how I feel about my career, how you dealt with your problem with . . .)

How much time do you spend on each of these categories during a typical working week — represent this on a pie chart using a symbol or colour for each.

Does the way you structure your time give you the quality of contact you want with others?

How predictable are the structures you have at work? First, what are the most important structures at work for you? Note down those which are relevant to you:

1. Regular meetings with . . . (Which people? How often? What kind of topics are important? Formal or informal?)

2. Reporting relationships. (Organization structure/chart. Which relationships are particularly important for you?)

3. Physical environment. (Layout of offices; distance from boss; personal space; lighting; ventilation; 'neighbours', distance from car parks, station, bus stop, shops, bank, etc.)

4. Procedures, systems. (Office or professional procedures and systems important to you; from who opens the post to who signs it, from how to get a photocopy to getting a major decision made.)

5. Professional or traditional practices. (Those which are important to you in the organization or your profession.)

6. Other structures. (e.g., security of job, pension arrangements.)

Which of those which are important to you have changed in the last year? Which will change in the next year?

How can you build in the kind of structure you want in your life, even when the organization changes?

Exercise 3.5 Frustration and getting what you want: Variety and stimulation

Three words are relevant here: fun, satisfaction and excitement. Fun, satisfaction and excitement may come from a single activity, e.g. you may enjoy making a major presentation because it is fun preparing for it and meeting people; you may get a sense of satisfaction from persuading people to your view; and you may find it exciting because it is an opportunity to exercise your skill and turn a difficult audience into an enthusiastic one. On the other hand you may find that you mostly get fun, satisfaction and excitement from different activites; perhaps fun is reserved for home and lunch-breaks, satisfaction comes from clearing your in-tray, and excitement from pushing yourself to the limits of your professional capacity or arguing with colleagues.

What sorts of decisions did you make about fun, satisfaction and excitement when you were young?

Do any of them seem relevant to the way you work now?

What activities at work do you have fun doing?

What activities at work do you get a sense of satisfaction from?

What activities at work do you get excitement from?

Do you get enough of each *for you?*

Are any of these activities *unsafe* for you? (Do they, for example, stop you getting what you want in other areas of your life, or stop you getting positive recognition, or perhaps even mean that you may end up sacked or demoted or pushed sideways?) This question particularly applies to the activities which give you excitement.

Think about people you know at work whom you respect. How do you imagine they get fun, satisfaction and excitement at work?

Are there any elements in your answer to the last question which you could *safely* incorporate in your model for yourself?

Exercise 3.6 *How you create your mammoths*

Now review each of your modern-day mammoths (see Ex. 3.1) in turn. What is it about each which concerns you? What are the messages that you give yourself when you face or are about to face them? What are the unhelpful parts of your internal conversation?

Then identify an alternative view which you could incorporate to help modify your perception of these as threats.

	Modern mammoths	Reason for perception of threat	Alternative way of perceiving situation
Example	Missing a deadline (even though I have too much work)	Whatever the personal cost I should have tried harder and worked faster to get it done. I failed to do so.	I was unable to finish everything; I could have been clearer about priorities and I'll do that next time.
	1.		
	2.		
	3.		

4. Developing skills for dealing with pressure: Facing up to mammoths

In the last chapter we focused on re-evaluating perceptions of situations and people to see if they really are threatening. Even when you have re-evaluated your view of the pressures you face you will still encounter some difficult situations; and you will need skills for dealing with the many events which create pressure for you. In this chapter we will focus on a vital set of skills for dealing with modern-day mammoths.

These skills are an essential ingredient of your survival guide. It is tempting to try to manage pressure by focusing only on those factors which produce it. This is one strategy available to you, but you can also increase your ability to cope. In this chapter we will look at assertion as a key skill for dealing with difficult events.

In any situation there are a number of options open to you. We believe that assertiveness is the style most appropriate for dealing with people in threatening situations. In this chapter we will not be prescribing precisely what you should do or say; instead, we will be focusing on *how* you speak and *how* you act. There are three reasons for this. First, how you say things and do things will have a marked effect on how you feel at the end of an encounter with a difficult person. Second, how you say and do things will have a marked effect on other people. Third, how you say things and do things will affect whether you achieve your aims and objectives. So, by speaking and acting assertively you gain three benefits when under pressure: you feel better; you are likely to have better relations with others; and you are more likely to achieve your targets.

Assertiveness is an important skill when you face mammoths:
- Because if you are assertive you can learn to handle mammoths better. For example, you can learn that when you disagree skilfully with your manager at a team meeting, none of the imagined serious consequences actually come about.
- Because if you are assertive and deal with each small event one at a time, the overall impact of accumulated small events is lessened. For example, if you have already dealt effectively with a stream of difficult customers and clients the next difficult encounter to come along brings

less pressure than if the previous difficulties have not been satisfactorily resolved.

- Because if you are assertive you can say no to inappropriate, unrealistic or excessive demands. In standing up for yourself effectively you can also help your staff. Saying no appropriately means that there is less pressure around. For example, one manager explained how he had been asked to do a very large piece of work. He recognized that this would put a lot of pressure on him and his staff, but felt unable to refuse because he could see that it was important. However, when he realized the implications of doing the work and the consequences for him and his staff, he did in fact say no to his manager in an appropriate way. He explained what the problems were. His manager simply said, 'That's fine, I'll find extra staff and somebody else to do it.' It was not a problem in the end. Yet saying no to his boss had seemed like a 'mammoth' to him.

Below are listed some examples of forms of assertiveness which are useful for dealing with mammoths:

- Saying no to inappropriate or unfair requests.
- Speaking up at meetings and making sure your views are heard.
- Feeling comfortable about expressing your opinions if you disagree with someone else's views.
- Being able to accept or go along with a decision someone else has made, knowing that you have put your case well.
- Being able to accept criticism and praise when they are constructive.
- Being able and willing to give constructive criticism and praise.
- Being able to handle snubs or people putting you down without starting a fight.
- Facing difficult decisions, not running away from them.

What you can do when facing a mammoth: Four styles of coping

The importance of the way in which you say and do things can be demonstrated by looking at the different ways of saying no to an inappropriate request or unfair demand. You can say no simply by not doing it. You can say, 'I do not really want to, but I suppose if you insist I will.' You can say, 'No, I jolly well won't do it. I don't care what your problems are right now, I am not going to do it.' You can say, 'I am not prepared to take that bit of work on, let's see if there is any other way that we can get it done.' Only the last of these is an assertive response. We want now to contrast assertiveness with the other styles available to you.

Let's use the example of a physical threat and look at the options that are available. We will then see how those options relate to behaviour at work.

Imagine that as you are walking home one evening you round a rather dark corner and notice a figure in the shadows ahead of you. You continue on your way but begin to wonder whether this person has good intentions. The person turns to face you and pulls out a flick-knife. By now your chemical orchestra is probably in full swing. If you were to stop and take note of the state of your body you would notice that your heart was racing, you were breathing rapidly, you were probably beginning to sweat, and so on.

The physiological reaction to a threat is to prepare for fight or flight and, indeed, as you quickly assess the situation you might decide to fight. You may decide on the other hand, that you are going to run away as fast as you can.

There are in fact two other courses of action open to you. The first of these is to freeze and keep totally still. The whole chemical orchestra might be activated but you neither run nor fight. You go into a frozen state in which your legs do not move or in which you open your mouth and nothing comes out. The fourth option open to you, other than fight, flight or freeze, is to talk your way out of the situation. You could calmly ask what the person wants and listen to the response, with the intention of reaching a compromise.

In this situation what you actually do may not *feel* like a choice because your reaction will be so fast. It is a choice, however, and — reading the above — you have probably formed a view about which choice you would make in this circumstance. Each of the options has advantages and disadvantages. Of course at work you do not face many muggers but when you face one of your personal mammoths the same options are available. In order to increase your skill in assertive behaviour you need to be clear how it differs from the fight, flight or freeze options. The labels given to the four styles we have just identified are aggressive, unassertive, passive and assertive behaviour. These styles refer to the way you deal with other people. We are not implying that the people you deal with necessarily pose a threat to you, but, in organizations, difficult situations usually involve dealing with others.

Read through the examples which follow and identify in each of them the unassertive, aggressive, passive and assertive response. This will help you to get a clearer idea of the differences between these behaviours. Focus on identifying the style by the kinds of words used and the tone of the example.

Example 1: The buck stops here

Imagine the following scene. You come into your office and find that someone is waiting to see you. He is very angry and upset and seems intent on blaming you as the manager for something that has gone wrong. He seems to be looking for a fight. Possible reactions are:

  – Saying he is right, before you know all the facts, in order to pacify him; offering an apology and promising to put it right, while at the same time wishing it had not happened as you have so much to do.

- Averting your eyes and looking down at the floor while saying nothing, hoping that he will soon run out of steam and go away.
- Immediately joining in the fight by being sarcastic and intimating that the person has probably got himself into this mess and that it is not your fault; interrupting him to state your opinion, without finding out the facts first, and generally taking the offensive.
- Calmly asking for the person's view of what has happened, gleaning the facts and agreeing with those you know to be the case; making a note of the problem and further information you will need; showing that you can see that he is angry and upset; asking what he wants you to do and agreeing a future course of action.

Example 2: The incomplete report

You are confronted by a colleague who wants to know why a report she wants is not already completed. Some of the possible responses include:

- Saying that you are terribly sorry and that you will stay late to finish it, that you are really rather inexperienced at this sort of thing and after all she did ask for that other report only yesterday and it really is all rather difficult. (All this will probably be said as you slowly edge away from her.)
- Bowing your head, with hands clasped together as the words reverberate around you, offering no reason or explanation, merely waiting for the storm to abate.
- Saying that you have been very busy with all the other things that she has asked for and that it is a bit much, even if she thinks it is important; she ought to know you have got more important things to do, and it is about time she realized that you have no intention of being at her beck and call; she should sort it out herself if she wants it. (All of this is said with chin thrust forward and hands on hips.)
- Saying that you appreciate that it is important for her, that it is your top priority today and will be finished as agreed tomorrow morning. However, since she has asked for the report and seems concerned about it, this seems like a good opportunity to talk about your workload to see if you can agree some changes as you are under a lot of pressure at the moment. (While you are talking you are standing in such a way that you can look straight at her in a relaxed way.)

In each of these cases, the first response is the unassertive one, the second passive, the third aggressive, and the last one assertive. They are not the only possible responses, but examples of the four coping styles. The first step in developing the skill of assertiveness is recognizing assertive behaviour as contrasted with the other options. The second step is to recognize how your beliefs affect your choice of behaviour. Any beliefs which are incompatible with assertive behaviour will tend to 'leak' through into your behaviour. Developing your assertive style is easier if you look at beliefs as well as behaviour.

Beliefs underlying the four styles of coping

As should be clear from the above examples, the unassertive style entails failing to stand up for yourself and for your department. You are discounting yourself as a manager by acting in a pacifying way, taking the blame and responsibility for something that may not be your fault, and offering to do something which goes against what you in fact want. In neither example of an unassertive response is the real problem actually tackled. The behaviours are aimed at appeasing. The rationale is that in some way I am not capable of dealing with a threat, so I may as well give in and hope others will not attack me. 'I lose and you win' is the strategy for survival.

By using the passive behaviour the person takes no action, or as little as possible. No moves are taken to deal with the problem, not even to avoid it. Behind this lies the belief that I cannot deal with a threat, so I will make myself as unobstrusive as possible and hope that no one notices me; I do not believe anyone else can do anything constructive either. This is a no-win position.

The aggressive style of dealing with people is active, but the behaviour is aimed at removing the problem by attacking and defeating the other person. This behaviour does not take account of the person's needs even to the extent of recognizing that they have a problem. There is little attempt to treat the other person with courtesy and little recognition that he or she matters. This style is based on the assumption that if I win, you must lose, because I believe I can only get what I want if you don't.

In the unassertive responses the implication is that I am in some way inferior to the person I am dealing with. The implication in the passive responses is that really the situation is hopeless. It is not that the person is inferior, rather that neither party can really do a great deal. In the aggressive style the implication is that I am superior in some way.

In the assertive option in both of the above examples, the person clearly treats the other as an equal. This may cut across the hierarchy of relationships in organizations. The key point is not whether one person is superior or subordinate to the other in the hierarchy, but whether one acts in a superior or inferior manner towards the other. The assertive style adopts neither the superior, the inferior nor the hopeless stance; it assumes the two people are *equal as people.* Regardless of any hierarchical relationship they treat each other with respect. That does not mean in either of the two examples that the manager does exactly what the other person wants, nor does it mean that he or she tries to discount the other person's wants. Instead the assertive style recognizes that both people have a problem that needs to be solved and that it can best be solved cooperatively. The essence of the assertive style is mutuality and interdependence. This means recognition that in a social system of any kind we need each other's assistance. The aim is to go for a solution in which I win and so do you. Both of us can get something of what we want. I will stand up for myself but give your views weight.

Having read through these examples, you may think that the assertive style is one that you find easy to use. Many people, however, will recognize the unassertive, passive and aggressive style either as their habitual approach or as the style they use when under pressure. It is difficult to assert yourself under pressure, even if you manage to be assertive the rest of the time. Chapter 2 showed that people are programmed physiologically for fight or flight, and under pressure people's first resort is usually to use modern-day equivalents: aggression and unassertive/passive behaviour.

Whilst it may be appropriate in some circumstances to be aggressive, unassertive or passive with people, we believe that in the long run the assertive option is the most effective. This will certainly be the case when a relationship extends over time or needs to improve and develop, for it is based on the assumption that both parties can get what they want and are of equal value as people. The two sides may not be equal in terms of hierarchical position, skills, ability or experience, but both are viewed as important *as people.* If there is some difficulty with a relationship, the assertive option will be the one most likely to permanently diffuse the threat. Problems with the other person will be dealt with as problems not threats. Passive, unassertive and aggressive styles may help you survive in the short term, but will not lead to effective relations with others in the long term.

How to be assertive

Assertive behaviour has two elements: verbal behaviour (your choice of words and phrases); and non-verbal behaviour or body language (your choice of gestures, body posture, facial expression). These two elements are all that others can observe and will influence their response to you.

Your ability to be assertive is not simply dependent on your ability to mimic but on the beliefs and thoughts and feelings you have about particular situations; the specific inner dialogue you have when you face a difficult situation. When, in certain situations, you find it difficult to exercise the verbal and non-verbal aspects of assertion, it is likely that your beliefs or thoughts about the situation are getting in the way of exercising that skill.

What to say and how to say it

We will now examine some of the verbal and non-verbal aspects of assertion and compare them with aggressive, unassertive and passive behaviour. Table 4.1 shows some examples of the differences between these four behaviours.

	Assertive	Unassertive	Aggressive	Passive
Verbal content	– Statements clear, brief and to the point – 'I' statements – Distinction between facts and opinion – No 'shoulds' and 'oughts' – Constructive criticism – Questions to get facts – Looking for solutions – Pauses to let others in – States wants clearly	– Apologizes a great deal and effusively – Dismisses own needs – Puts self down – Frequent justifications for own behaviour – Few 'I' statements – Qualifiers (just, sort of…) – Uh, umm… – Questions to find out what others want – Anticipates	– Excess 'I' statements – Boastfulness – Possessiveness ('my') – Opinions and fact confused – Threatening questions, requests or instructions – Sarcasm – Puts down others – Interrupts – Talks over others	– Responds to others monosyllabically – Dismissive of own and others' ideas – Seems to have difficulty concentrating on the meaning of conversations – Asks few questions, appears uninterested in others – Preoccupied
Non-verbal content	– Steady, firm voice – Neither loud nor soft voice – Modulated tone – Fluent – Steady pace – Open reaction — smiles when pleased, frowns when angry – Firm gaze – Open movements – Head erect – Relaxed	– Wobbly voice – Quiet voice – Hesitant – Frequent throat clearing – Evasive look – Looking down – Hiding parts of body, e.g. hands in pockets or hand over mouth – Hunched shoulders – Hand wringing – Crossed, protective arms – Some muscles tense	– Very firm tone – Cold/sarcastic – Strident/loud voice – Fluent – Abrupt – Speaks fast – Scowls – Chin forward – Stares others down – Finger-pointing – Fist-thumping/ clenched fists – Arms crossed (unapproachable) – Some muscles tense	– Flat voice – Often monotone – Sentences trail off unfinished – Glassy-eyed, unfocused look – Immobile expression – Little movement – Tense all over, rigid – Quiet

Table 4.1 Showing examples of verbal and non-verbal elements of assertive, unassertive, aggressive and passive behaviour

It is important to emphasize that assertive behaviour is not cold and unfeeling as is sometimes imagined. You will of course experience strong feelings in difficult situations. The point is that you have a choice as to how to express those feelings, or indeed whether to express them at all. You can, for example, express your feelings in an aggressive way, by blaming others, using sarcasm or adopting a punitive tone. If you choose to be unassertive you may direct your feelings inwards at yourself. An example of this is feeling guilty and blaming yourself even if you are not responsible. If you use the passive style there will be little if any expression of the feelings involved. Alternatively you can express your feelings openly in an appropriate way — this is being assertive. It means saying how you feel in a way which is direct, neither punitive nor masochistic, and addressed to the appropriate person. This applies to any feelings, whether you are feeling scared, anxious, excited, angry or whatever. Even if you do not express your feelings directly they will often show in your behaviour.

The assertive style is one in which you face up to the situation directly and openly, and carefully choose the appropriate words for describing what you are thinking or how you are feeling. Unassertive behaviour is a protective and defensive strategy, and the gestures and phrases associated with the unassertive style are also defensive and protective. The passive style is also intended to protect but in this case it is the lack of reaction, the lack of movement, which forms the defensive strategy and so all gestures and phrases are 'flattened' and unobtrusive. The aggressive style is challenging in a hostile way rather than constructively challenging. This distinction can be difficult to make at times, as assertive people frequently challenge assumptions or beliefs with the aim of getting more information and trying to tease out the different factors involved. A person being aggressive treats situations as competitive rather than co-operative. This will be noticeable in the gestures, postures and words used.

Exercise 4.1 at the end of the chapter helps you link the verbal and non-verbal aspects of assertion to your own experience.

Using assertive behaviour when you need to

Having identified assertive behaviour the next problem is how to use those particular behaviours, both verbal and non-verbal, at the time when you need them. We find it helpful to use the analogy of pressing the 'pause button' either before going into a situation or before speaking. You can change the whole course of a conversation by using your pause button because it gives you time to become aware of what you are thinking and feeling. You then have the time to monitor yourself and make decisions about what you will say in response to others and how you will say it, rather than responding automatically in your habitual way. The key factor is how you use the time you give yourself and what you do once you have pressed the pause button. Figure 4.1, the behavioural diamond, illustrates how you can use the pause button and choose assertive behaviour.

One of the keys to using the pause button effectively is the inner dialogue, which we look at in the next section. Once you have developed your skills using the first four exercises at the end of the chapter, Ex. 4.5 will help you develop your 'pause button' technique.

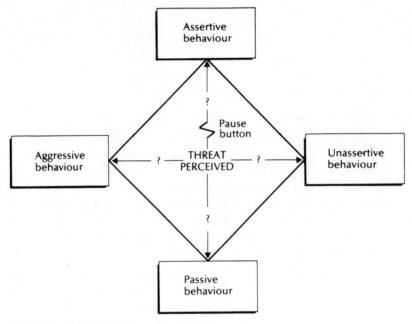

Figure 4.1 The behavioural diamond

How to talk yourself into being assertive: The inner dialogue

Beliefs and values are central to our inner dialogue, which influences not only the perception of threat but also how it is dealt with. In Chapter 3 we discussed the importance of a review of your central beliefs so that you can reduce pressure on yourself by avoiding inappropriate application of them. In developing the skill of assertion you need to review which beliefs you incorporate in your inner dialogue in *specific situations,* so that you can avoid inappropriate or faulty thinking. Faulty thinking influences your use of the four behaviours and inhibits assertion. Let's look at an example.

Imagine that one Saturday you bought an electric kettle. When you got home you discovered it had a fault and realized that you would need to go back and exchange it. You decided that you wanted your money back or a replacement. Now imagine that you are driving back to the shop the following Saturday. If you listen to the inner dialogue you are having with yourself it might sound like this:

- The last time I had to deal with this shop I was angry at the way I was treated. In fact, I bet that if I am not very careful they will treat me like that again. I remember that the manager was not helpful; and she should be, it's her job. I remember having a real stand-up row. I suppose I had better prepare myself for another row like that. I ought to stand up to her. I am going to stand my ground and make sure that when I go in there I am not walked all over.

By the time you get to the shop the chances are that when you speak to the manager you will say something along the lines of, 'Look, I don't care what you say, I demand to have this replaced immediately and I am not putting up with any nonsense.'

Alternatively you may be saying to yourself:

- I do hate taking things back. I always feel as if it is my fault that it has gone wrong. I bet there is just something wrong with my wiring of the plug. I ought to be careful not to upset people, after all it's just a kettle. There will be lots of people watching as well, and I mustn't look foolish. The manager will probably not be at all helpful anyway and will just tell me that they will take it away and repair it. Anyway, if it were repaired it would not be too bad. I would prefer to be able to take a new one away with me now, but a repair would not be too bad.

If that were the inner dialogue you would probably walk into the shop and say to the manager something like, 'Um… I hope you don't mind me bringing this back but I bought it last week and it does not seem to work. I wonder if you could repair it for me?'

Another conversation you could be having with yourself is:

- I remember last time that I did not have much success with this manager who was very unhelpful. I will not let that get in the way of what happens this time. I will be clear about what I want. I want either my money back or a replacement. I know that I have a right to ask for that. I will not be fobbed off with a repair, I will stick to my ground firmly and politely. I will not rise to the bait if the manager acts in the same way as last time and is unhelpful. I will ask for what I want.

In that case you would probably go up to the counter and explain what the problem is by saying something like, 'I bought this last week and it is not working. I would like a replacement. If you have not got a replacement in stock, I would like you to refund my money.' This is probably the most helpful way of opening up that particular conversation.

Using this example you can see how your inner dialogue affects the choices you make about actions. Your inner dialogue may relate to your early learning. If you decided, when a child, to stand up for yourself because you had concluded that the world was a dangerous place, it will then be quite normal for you to go in with a fighting inner dialogue. This can be changed at two levels. The early decisions about the world can be reviewed, and then the inner dialogue for each particular situation can be changed. Changing the inner dialogue means changing the way you think.

The first stage is to identify the inner dialogue you are having at a particular moment. The second stage is to challenge it, to check whether it is a sound or faulty dialogue in terms of what you are trying to achieve. The third stage is to replace faulty dialogue with sound dialogue. Exercise 4.2 at the end of the chapter helps you practise identifying different kinds of inner dialogues and choosing assertive dialogues and responses.

In Table 4.2 you will find two examples of challenging the inner dialogue, checking whether it is flawed, and replacing it with sound inner dialogue.

You can extend the technique of challenging the inner dialogue to help you prepare for a difficult encounter. Predict the problems you expect to face, based on your knowledge of the person, and construct a sound inner dialogue for dealing with the predicted problems. Identify the assertive behaviour you want to use. You will then have a sound inner dialogue and assertive responses worked out and even rehearsed in advance.

Building the confidence to be assertive

The more confident you feel the easier you will find it to be assertive, because you are less likely to perceive situations as threatening, and therefore less likely to use unassertive, passive or aggressive behaviour. The more often you are assertive the less pressure you will experience and therefore the less vulnerable you will be. Because you are less vulnerable you will feel less pressure and therefore will find it easier to be assertive.

Realistic self-confidence is not the same as arrogance. Arrogance is an inflated view of your strengths and a deflated view of your weaknesses in dealing with problems. Nor is realistic self-confidence the same as false modesty, which is an inflated view of your weaknesses and a deflated view of your strengths. Self-confidence involves being realistic, basing your assessment of yourself on actual evidence. Based on your experiences in the past and your achievements and failures, you will have expectations of what you can achieve in similar situations in the future. Self-confidence is a realistic assessment of the probability of success in the situations you face.

Self-confidence is an important factor underlying the skill of assertion. If you do not believe that you can deal with a difficulty skilfully then your chances of doing so are remote.

The most effective way of developing your confidence is through a carefully planned programme designed to improve your skills of assertion. Your confidence will grow as you become more practised at being assertive. If you practise using the new skills with small difficulties, eventually you will have confidence to deal with the large ones.

Developing realistic self-confidence: Practising the skills of assertion

If you are skilled at using the assertive style your scope for development will be marginal. If, however, you feel uneasy at choosing this style and find it difficult to

	What is my inner dialogue at the moment?	Challenges – is this dialogue faulty?	What will be my sound inner dialogue?	What are my feelings?	What initial assertion am I going to make
Example 1	In the last project meeting I really came off badly. I looked very foolish when I didn't have the figures to back my claim. I'll have to really show them who's boss this time, or I'll lose my grip on the whole project. I'll have to put everyone in their place whenever they challenge my authority.	Did I really look foolish to others? Is this the way to get real respect from the team? Do I have the right to put others down because I made a mistake?	I'll make sure I have all the detail I need this time. I'll be open about last time by reintroducing the problem, providing the data and chairing the open discussion. They have the right to put their views and be listened to. I have the responsibility to choose the best option after the discussion.	A bit anxious about how it'll go and whether I'll handle it well. No longer angry with *them* for something *I* did.	I want to return to an item from last week which we couldn't deal with then. I have the figures now, and they're not as hopeful as I had expected. What do each of you think we should do now we have these figures?
Example 2	Oh dear, a meeting about my proposal. She read the report, why does she have to go through it again? She must think it's hopeless. I hope the points she makes aren't too fundamental. Probably a disaster and she will expect the whole thing reworked. She's probably biased anyway.	Does a meeting automatically mean disapproval? What previous evidence do I have for this? Am I worrying about this report or something else? Why do I assume she'll challenge the basis of my proposal? Did I stick to the brief? Do I have any evidence of bias?	I was pleased with my ideas and I have confidence in them. I spoke with her in general terms and she was happy, so it's probably to go through the detail. Even if she questions my report I can substantiate my case. There's no a priori reason to see it as a disaster. It's OK not to get everything perfect. She's never shown bias before.	OK. Curious about her opinion of my work. Comfortable at the prospect of going through it with her. No longer vacillating between scared and angry.	I'm interested to know how you react to my report. I'm pleased with the ideas of mine which I've incorporated and wonder now how they came across to you?

Table 4.2 Challenging the inner dialogue

be assertive, there will be more room for improvement. Developing any new skill takes time and effort. You will not get it right nor act in the way you planned every time, but gradually it will become a more familiar skill and one you can exercise in more and more difficult circumstances.

As you practise any new skill there are times when it feels as though you are not improving. Indeed, it can feel as though you have actually got worse. If you persist, however, eventually your level of skill will improve.

In developing the skill of assertion you are aiming to develop a virtuous circle of success, rather than a vicious circle of failure. To do this you need to make two separate assessments. The first is an assessment of the situation you face and the second is an assessment of yourself. You need both of these to choose the most suitable circumstances for practising the skill you are developing. This is very important because practising the skill of assertion in a situation in which you do not succeed can result in a loss of confidence.

To assess the situation, it is useful to ask yourself whether it is luck or skill which determines success or failure in this circumstance. How much personal control do you have over the outcome? For example, if you are worried about a reorganization which has been decided by an executive board of directors, and you go to see your boss who is a middle-ranking manager to ask that the reorganization should not affect you and that your special circumstances be taken into account, your manager may not be able to help, however skilfully you put your case. This is because he or she has very little input into the decisions taken at board level. Neither you nor your manager has much power to alter that set of decisions. However skilfully you operate, it is unlikely that the particular encounter between the two of you will affect the outcome.

If, on the other hand, you want to undertake a particular piece of work which is within your manager's gift, and you speak to your manager and do so skilfully, the way you put your case will be an important determinant of whether or not you get the work. There is a much greater chance of success in this case, and so it is worth practising your skills of assertion. In the first case it is not realistic to attempt to persuade your manager, let alone use the situation to build your confidence.

The second dimension is your assessment of your own level of skill. In particular there may be some kinds of situation and some people with whom you know you have difficulty asserting yourself. If you feel that your assertive skill is not very well developed yet, it is entirely inappropriate to practise on those situations at the beginning. It is more appropriate to find situations which are challenging for you but at the same time do not carry serious consequences if you are not totally successful in asserting yourself. Tackling your boss on a major problem that you have been avoiding for some time may not be the ideal situation in which to practise your developing skill.

The sense of self-confidence that you develop through knowledge of your strengths and past successes can be incorporated in your inner dialogue. Remind yourself of how you succeeded in a similar situation last time. Remind yourself that, although you are not good at everything, you do have strengths. Exercise 4.3 will help you to practise your skill in sensible ways and offers a framework for thinking through your preparation.

Hints for exercising the skill of assertion

Table 4.3 provides some hints to help you exercise the skill of assertion. Pick out the ones relevant to you and incorporate them in your handling of the sort of situations described. There are hints for protecting yourself from aggressive people assertively, disagreeing with others assertively, refusing requests assertively, and giving praise and criticism assertively. If you find that any of these hints are very unfamiliar Ex. 4.4 at the end of the chapter is a good way of incorporating them before you go on to use them in practise.

Table 4.3 Hints for developing assertive skills

Protecting yourself from aggressive people

Show the person that you understand what he or she is saying. You can do this, for example, by saying, 'I can see that you're very angry about what happened at the meeting. You still sound pretty cross about it.' Making it clear that you recognize how the other person is feeling doesn't mean that you agree with his or her arguments, or that you feel the same. It is merely saying that you recognize the strength of the feelings that he or she is expressing.

Listen to what the person is saying and pick out the arguments. If there is some truth in them, agree with those facts, but not with all the person is saying, and without making a grovelling apology. If, for example somebody says to you, 'You're an absolute idiot, you got half the information wrong at that meeting. Honestly, I don't know where you got it from at all', your response might be, 'It's true that I did have some incorrect information on the March figures.' You don't have to agree that you're an idiot, and you don't have to comment on the person's statement that he or she doesn't know where you got the information from, because that is a rhetorical device, a way of putting you down, rather than a factual argument. Try to stick to dealing with the facts.

Ask what the person wants of you, or tell them what, if anything, you are prepared to do; for example 'I'm prepared to send a memo round with the right figures to those concerned. Do you think this will be helpful?' You don't have to agree, again, to everything the other demands of you, like admitting to being an idiot; you must feel comfortable with whatever you offer.

Rehearse your own rights in this situation. Is it reasonable for you to have made a mistake and, if so, do you have the responsibility for putting it right? Does the other person have a right to expect you to put it right? If so, that reinforces the action you will take now to rectify your mistake.

Disagreeing with others

State your disagreement clearly. ('No, I disagree with....' 'I don't go along with....')

Express your doubts constructively. ('Will that lead to...?' 'The difficulty I foresee is....' 'Can we get around it?') Don't be woolly about your disagreement or simply say, 'That won't work. We've tried it before and it didn't work.'

Distinguish your opinion from fact. ('As I see it....' 'I believe....' 'My experience is....')

Be willing to change your opinion in the light of new information. ('In view of what you've just said I can see....')

Consider whether you need to give reasons for your disagreement. This is particularly important if you've said, 'That won't work.' If you've just left it at, 'No, I don't go along with that', or 'I disagree with that', then there is less need to give reasons for your disagreement, but if you have voiced an objection then it is useful to be able to back it up.

Recognize other people's points of view. ('I appreciate that it affects you differently', or 'I understand that you see things in a different light, and I disagree or won't go along with....')

Refusing requests

Keep the reply short. Avoid long, rambling justifications. Simply say, 'No I don't want to', 'I prefer not to', 'I'd rather not', or 'I'm not happy to', rather than inventing an excuse.

Give a reason if you want to but, again, don't invent excuses. Give reasons if you think it will be helpful to you and the other person, but not as a justification or an explanation when you don't need to give one.

Avoid 'I can't' because it sounds like an excuse and as though you're not responsible for your own actions. Instead, say 'I won't', 'I'm not prepared to', or 'I'm not going to'.

Don't apologize profusely. If you do want to say you're sorry because you genuinely sympathize with the other person, simply say that. Don't make an apology into a grovelling excuse.

Ask for more information, if you need it, before deciding whether or not to refuse the request, but don't ask for more information simply as a way of avoiding making a decision about whether or not to refuse a request.

Acknowledge the person who's made the request. ('It's kind of you to ask, but I don't want to go to that meeting as the issues I want to discuss aren't on the agenda.')

Show warmth and attentiveness to the person making the request so that he or she understands that your refusal is not because you haven't heard what he or she has been saying, or because you have no concern for him or her as a person. Your refusal is a refusal of the request, not a rejection of the individual.

Giving praise and criticism

Comment on specific actions. (For example, 'You handled that awkward customer very well', rather than, 'Generally speaking, you're quite good with difficult people aren't you?' or, 'You missed the deadline for that report', rather than, 'You're absolutely hopeless at managing your time.')

Follow this up with reasons for your comments. This is helpful whether the comments are positive or negative because we need to know what we are being praised for if we are to take the praise as being genuine and to know how to use it as helpful feedback. ('The reason I think you handled that awkward customer very well was because you asked her what her complaint was, you took down the details and you explained clearly what we would do to put it right.' 'You missed the deadline for that report. I think the reason you missed the deadline is that you have spent more time on telephone sales than we planned and yet it was important to get that report in. I'd like to discuss with you how you allocate your time.')

Specifically when you're giving praise, don't seek to put a mortgage on the future. Don't make your praise a carrot to encourage people to work harder or do difficult tasks for you in the near future. ('You're the most hardworking member of staff I've got. I really appreciate the effort you've put in. I imagine that you can probably finish this little job off before you go home this evening, can't you?') Praise is accepted as such if it is seen as a response to better-than-usual performance and not as a way of manipulating people into doing something for you.

When giving criticism, specifically describe the facts of the problem with a view to seeking solutions rather than seeking to comment on somebody's personality. 'You're getting far too many complaints from members of the public recently. What the heck's the matter with you anyway?' is not a very helpful form of criticism. It is much more helpful to say something like, 'You seem to be having complaints from members of the public in your section at the moment. I wonder what is going on.' Avoid public put-downs when giving criticism. Find an opportunity to discuss the problem in such a way that you are not simply doling out criticism. Your approach should suggest that you want to solve the problem, rather than put the other person down.

A framework for developing the skill of assertion

Figure 4.2 (on page 52) shows a framework for developing the skill of assertion. By now we hope that you have a good grasp of the basic ideas and choices open to you for dealing with modern-day mammoths. You now need to practise the verbal skills, the non-verbal skills and the inner dialogue. Finally you need to put all these elements together in an integrated assertive approach to difficult situations. The exercises which follow help you to understand the choices and practise your assertive skills.

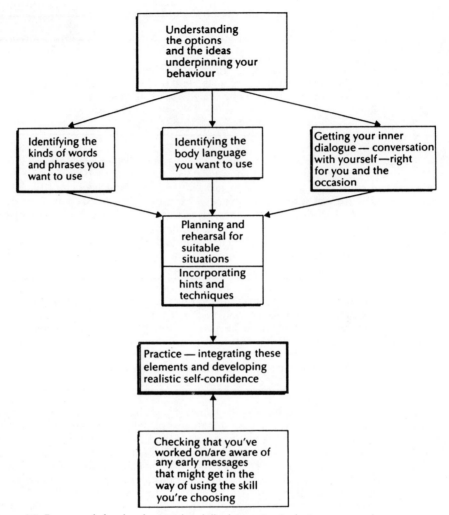

Figure 4.2 Framework for developing the skill of assertion in facing mammoths

Exercises for Chapter 4: Developing an assertive style for dealing with modern-day mammoths

Exercise 4.1 Recognizing the four styles of behaviour

In this exercise we focus on how to recognize the four styles — unassertive, aggressive, assertive and passive — in the verbal and non-verbal behaviours that you can see and hear people use. Being able to identify the elements of each will help you to choose the assertive style more easily. Although we've included some examples in Table 4.1, this exercise is for you to develop your own lists of key features.

First, think of someone you know at work who frequently uses *aggressive behaviour.* Think about how this person conducts him or herself. What kinds of words does he or she use which you think typify his or her aggressive behaviour? What phrases? What body language and tone of voice? Include posture, gestures and facial expressions. Write your observations in a table like that shown here. If you have an opportunity, check your observations the next time you see this person behaving aggressively.

The second step is to focus on yourself. When you use aggressive behaviour, what are the words and phrases you most frequently use? What kinds of body language do you use? If you have a colleague or friend you can cross-check with him or her; it is often helpful to get someone else's view.

Now repeat these two steps for the other three styles.

		Aggressive	Unassertive	Passive	Assertive
SELF	*verbal (words and phrases)*				
	non-verbal (gestures, facial expressions, tone of voice, posture)				
OTHERS	*verbal (words and phrases)*				
	non-verbal (gestures, facial expressions, tone of voice, posture)				

Exercise 4.2 *Inner dialogues: Conversations with yourself*

In this exercise we focus on the kinds of internal conversations which are likely to end in assertive, unassertive, aggressive or passive responses.

In each example we give the internal dialogue for one of the styles, and we suggest that you fill in the others so that you get a feel for the kind of things you might say to yourself which would be likely to lead to one style of behaving or another. Then (Situation 5) think of a situation of your own. What would the assertive response to this situation be, and what might be the internal dialogue backing it up? Think about two or three situations in this way.

Situation 1

You hear that your manager has not been attending meetings with a group whose decisions could affect the future of the work of your section. She thinks the group is only concerned with politics.

	Response	*Internal dialogue*
Assertive	Explain the group's importance to a project you're working on and ask if she would agree to you attending some of the meetings as her deputy.	She has different priorities from me: that's OK. But it is important that this department is represented at these meetings. I'll find a way of solving this, so both of us feel OK.
Unassertive	Ask if you can help her out a bit more as there may then be more time for her to attend 'important meetings'.	
Aggressive	Ask her why others are letting the section down again.	
Passive	Do nothing.	

Situation 2

One of your members of staff requests an upgrading at his appraisal. His work is good and you've been considering doing this anyway. He then mentions a job interview he has and intimates that he'll drop it as soon as his upgrading is formalized.

	Response	*Internal dialogue*
Assertive	Tell him that you are considering the upgrading solely on the basis of the work he has done. You'd be sorry to lose him, but *he* must decide when it is the right time for him to look for another job.	
Unassertive	Tell him that you'll have to talk to your boss about it and you'll do it quickly. Tell him not to worry.	
Aggressive	Tell him not to threaten you and that he's got an inflated view of the quality of his work.	He's always too big for his boots. Well I'll take him down a peg or two. Who does he think he is anyway? Who's in charge of this appraisal interview?
Passive	Say that with the state of country as it is, it probably doesn't matter as we will all be redundant in the long run.	

Situation 3

A member of your staff says she hasn't had enough clear direction from you and asks for a long (half-day) session to get her job sorted out.

	Response	Internal dialogue
Assertive	'Thank you for being straight about this. I'd like us to get together and suggest we meet this week and sort out our agenda for a half-day meeting next week'.	
Unassertive	You send a memo clarifying your understanding of her job and ask her for her comments.	I can't face this meeting — she obviously doesn't think much of me as a manager. It'll be less threatening if we do it by memo. It will be less embarrassing for me.
Aggressive	You spend half an hour putting her right about how you see her job role and tell her to sleep on it.	
Passive	You laugh half-heartedly and say you're not sure what her job is either but if she wants a meeting it's OK by you.	

Situation 4

Your department has been involved in a major reorganization of administrative procedures including computerization. The company which is providing the software has been slow to produce the programmes, and its training procedures for staff are below standard.

	Response	Internal dialogue
Assertive	You decide to meet the senior manager from the company to clarify what you want and renegotiate the contract.	
Unassertive	You complain repeatedly to the people from the company who come to do the training. When your own boss asks what the hold-up is, you placate her with remarks like, 'We're all doing our best.'	
Aggressive	You phone up the company and speak to the MD. You bawl him out and slam the phone down.	
Passive	You commiserate with staff who are having trouble with the change-over. You try to avoid your boss whenever she asks you about progress by being 'unavailable'.	These big companies are all the same — it's no good tackling them because they don't really care and they won't listen. If we sit tight it'll come all right in the end, maybe.

Situation 5

Describe a situation of your own. We want you now to focus on the assertive response and internal dialogue.

	Response	Internal dialogue
Assertive		

Exercise 4.3 *Practising the assertive style of facing mammoths*

The first step is choosing a situation suitable for practice. The one you choose should be:

- One where personal skill and style will influence the outcome.
- Part of a progression, in your practising, from coping with less difficult situations to dealing with larger mammoths.

You can use role plays or 'real practice'.

Role plays

If you can find someone with whom you can practise, try acting out some of the situations you find difficult. You get the practise but the outcome doesn't matter.

You don't have to be a professional actor to do this. Simply be yourself and practise the skills you want to develop. Brief the other person as to how you want him or her to play his or her part. Role-play the encounter for five to ten minutes and then get the other person to discuss with you how you did. If there are three of you, one can observe the other two. Get your observer to be specific about the words and body language you used.

These one-line scenarios will get you started but go on to make up your own role plays based on *your* mammoths.

- Saying no to a drink offered by an important customer who is pressing you.
- Telling a colleague who keeps interrupting your work not to do so.
- Dealing with a member of your team whose quantity of work is excellent but whose quality of work is poor.
- Telling a member of staff that you're not recommending him or her for promotion.
- Telling your boss that constant interruptions from him or her about trivial matters are affecting your work.
- Disagreeing with another professional who starts a conversation with you by saying, 'As a fellow (engineer/psychologist/analyst/personnel professional/nurse/planner) of course you'll agree that....'

'Real practise'

Choose simple cases of a difficulty before you tackle your worst situation. For example, if your worst encounter is to be challenged professionally in a group of professional colleagues and you want to change your style for handling this, you might start by practising the skills in the office and *then* when you feel that they're becoming familiar and comfortable, practise them at the next meeting of your professional institute or association.

The second step is planning the encounter. This involves putting together the various elements of the skills that you have so far worked on separately.

As you develop your skills you will not need to do so much planning and will become better at exercising the skill spontaneously. The format shown here can be helpful for tricky occasions. One important point is that once you've done your planning and rehearsed the behaviour you want to try, you should put the proforma *away* until a few minutes before the encounter and forget it till then. There is no more planning that you can do.

Situation

(Who will be there, what I know about them, problem to be tackled, issues likely to be raised)

Behaviour I'll use

Verbal

Non-verbal

Behaviour I'll avoid

Verbal

Non-verbal

Inner dialogue

What am I thinking?

Is any of this thinking faulty or unsound or likely to lead to non-assertive behaviour?

What I'll replace it with (sound inner dialogue)

N.B. CHECK INNER DIALOGUE TAKES ACCOUNT OF SELF AND OTHER PEOPLE

Rehearsal

What is my initial assertion?

What difficulties do I predict?

How will I deal with these?

Monitor

How do I feel?

Am I realistically confident?

If not go back and work on this again. If so, put it away until the encounter.

Exercise 4.4 *Desensitizing yourself to mammoths*

This is similar in some respects to the previous exercise, but entails some clear visualization as well as imagination. It is particularly helpful when easier situations for practising the skills, such as role play, are unavailable. It takes you a stage further than the careful planning in which you rehearse what and how you will say your part. It involves visualizing reaching your goal, behaving as you would like to behave and experiencing how you feel when you do this.

In this technique, you visualize yourself in the scene you are concerned about. You do this not as though you're an actor watching yourself but as if you're really there. By visualizing yourself successfully dealing with the situation you will accustom yourself to the fact that you *can* feel differently in the presence of something or someone you used to see as a threat.

This is a good preparation for dealing effectively with the reality because in fantasy you have familiarized yourself with the feelings associated with exercising the skills.

Read through the instructions and then close your eyes to visualize clearly.

Choose a situation

The situation should be one in which you encounter one of your personal difficulties. Visualize it as if you are actually there.

Put the situation into a context

Where are you? Are you standing, sitting, lying? What can you feel next to your skin? Can you feel any pressures on your body? What is the place like? Look around you — what do you see? What do you smell? Is the air fresh or stale? How light is it? Can you touch anything? Who is there with you? What are they like? Are they standing? Sitting? How close are they? What are they saying or doing? How are they behaving towards you — pleased you're there, dismissive, or what? How do you feel? Be aware of your body, how you are holding yourself.

Decide what you want to do

What do you want out of this encounter? What would you like to do? What do you want the other(s) to say and do?

Use your skill

Now visualize yourself doing those things — *exactly* as you would like to. Imagine the other's response.

Rerun until you are happy

Did you do it as you wanted? Did the other(s) respond as you wanted? If not, go back and run the situation through again until you perfect the style you want to use and the outcomes you want. Change any aspects you don't like.

Be aware of how you feel. When you've run the scene as you like it, if you still do not feel familiar or comfortable with yourself in this role rerun again. When you are happy, open your eyes and return to the room you're in.

Exercise 4.5 Rethinking: How to deal with anticipating and reliving encounters with mammoths

One very common symptom of stress is sleeplessness. We do not need to be geared up physiologically to face a mammoth at 3 a.m. on a Monday morning when we do not meet it until Tuesday afternoon the following week! The longer before the event we start to anticipate it physically and mentally, and the longer after it has happened we let it go on affecting our levels of arousal, the more pressure we put on ourselves. The techniques of *rethinking* and *thought-stopping* are very helpful for countering the stress caused by anticipating and reliving encounters with mammoths.

Preparation is essential, whether the mammoth is a speech at a retirement party, organizing the office move, or any other event, but if the 'preparation' largely takes the form of panic, worry, over-rehearsal and sleeplessness then we are only preparing ourselves for struggle and tension, not for doing the job. So if the real preparation is done and nothing more can be achieved you need to stop going over it in your mind.

Rethinking

This is a version of changing the inner dialogue and using the 'pause button'. It consists of deliberately letting go of dead-end thoughts and allowing your emotions to subside as the thoughts go.

Imagine yourself getting frustrated because something you need has not been delivered as promised. You have planned your encounter with the salesperson from the supply company and 'phoned — only to find that he or she is out. You have been assured that this person will 'phone back within two hours. Instead of getting on with your work you are fretting and rehearsing what you will say. Complaining about poor service is a situation you really dislike.

Your internal dialogue runs something like: 'This is awful. Why did this have to happen today? They won't phone back — I'll have to phone again. I'll just go over it — I'll probably fly off the handle if I'm not careful', and so on.

When you hear yourself go through the 'This is awful' loop again, acknowledge your frustration by saying to yourself (out loud if possible): 'I am frustrated by this. I'm on edge. I'm cross about what happened and anxious about the next phone call.'

Then stop the 'This is awful' loop by saying (out loud if possible): 'No, this is not awful; it's merely what is happening here and now.'

Focus your mind on the reality of the situation and then on your next task. Useful conversations to have with yourself at this point may start with:
– What are the facts of the situation?
– What choices do I have at this point?
– How can I reorganize to meet this problem?

The technique is to acknowledge your feelings, stop repeating internal dialogue which fuels your anger or fright, and replace it with rational factual thought.

Thought-stopping

This is based on the idea that you need some trigger to stop you thinking the troublesome thoughts.

The simplest version of thought-stopping is to 'hear' in your mind the word 'stop!' being shouted loudly enough to interrupt the words you are thinking. This *interruption* can then be used to change the direction of thought by *substituting a new direction.* Replace the troublesome thoughts with pleasant ideas, images or sounds — sing a song, for example. If you don't substitute a new direction the chances are you will go back to the troublesome thoughts.

Get used to the sound of yourself shouting 'stop' by trying it out loud when you are alone. Hear yourself shouting 'stop' and memorize the sound you make.

The 'stop' shout is not the only trigger which can be used. You could, for example, 'hear' a few loud bars of a favourite symphony.

5. Making yourself fit to deal with pressure: Surviving mammoths

In the last chapter we looked at the skills of assertion which enable you to deal with the modern mammoths you meet. These skills will help you to keep your pressure at an optimum level. You also need to take into account the rate of wear and tear on your body. Living takes it out of you, and the final item you need in your survival guide is a strategy for reducing the effect of the pressure you experience. You need a lifestyle which maintains your fitness for dealing with pressure. Unfortunately many aspects of our modern lifestyle, far from helping us to stay fit, add to the pressure our bodies are facing. There is no single factor which will provide all-round protection; you need to take account of all aspects of your life and get them into balance. As there is no definitive list of mammoths, so there is no lifestyle which will suit everybody. This chapter is not about adding pressure by prescribing strict regimes. It is about adding to your survival guide items which suit you and which you enjoy.

A group of managers we met recently, for example, identified a wide range of items for reducing the rate of wear and tear in their lives. One decided to go for a five-mile run every morning. One thought that regular weekend retreats in the country would be helpful and decided to plan the next year to incorporate them. One focused on pleasurable and healthy eating habits and examined his current diet. Another decided that she needed to be more aware of what was happening to her and planned regular reviews of her life. The key point was that each person chose items which suited him or her.

We were interested in why these managers had not done anything so far to reorganize their lifestyles. After all, considerable media attention has been devoted to healthy living in recent years. In discussion with this and subsequent groups of managers we found that there were two main reasons why people found it difficult to develop healthy habits. First, they carry around many messages which get in the way of devising a healthy lifestyle. Second, many people, while wanting to improve their ability to cope with pressure, are not sure where to start or precisely what to do.

One way of summing up how to increase your ability to cope is to use the slogan devised by the Health Education Council, 'Look after yourself', but is it really that simple?

Messages which discourage us from looking after ourselves

In order to look after yourself you need to accept that it is permissible to devote time and attention to yourself. Unfortunately, many values and attitudes embedded in our culture contradict this. For example, there is a view held by many that it is a sign of weakness to expend effort on oneself.

The ease with which these cultural messages can be overcome is often linked to your own early learning. When you were young you received messages about your worth and value as a person. If those messages were positive you may well have formed the idea that you are important enough to warrant care and attention from others. You may or may not have also formed the notion that it is acceptable to pay attention to yourself.

While each person's early learning is unique, Table 5.1 shows some of the more common messages assimilated in the early years which either help or hinder taking care of yourself. You may need to replace some of the unhelpful messages you give yourself with helpful ones.

Unhelpful messages	Helpful messages
– Look after others; do not look after yourself.	– Look after yourself; then, if you want to, you will be better able to look after others.
– Your own needs are not important.	
– Looking after yourself is selfish.	– Looking after yourself is sensible.
– You are not worth looking after.	– You are worth while; you deserve attention.
– Other people are more important than you.	– Other people are important; you are important too.
– No grown person should want looking after.	– Everybody needs looking after sometimes.
– If you need looking after, hope someone will notice; don't ask.	– If you need looking after, be assertive with others and take care of your own needs.

Table 5.1 Messages that help or hinder taking care of yourself

Believing helpful messages such as those shown in Table 5.1 does not turn you into an uncaring, selfish, aggressive person. It is aggressive to consider your own needs at the expense of other people, but being unassertive, ignoring your own needs and focusing totally on the needs of others is not very sensible either. The aim is to look after yourself without ignoring or discounting those around you. It is not a matter of choosing between yourself and others. The fitter you are to deal with pressure yourself the more you will be able to help others constructively if you so choose. You can check on your attitudes to looking after yourself using Ex. 5.1 at the end of the chapter.

Why you need to look after yourself

As a manager you are responsible for the effectiveness of your staff. Most managers we talk to see their staff as their most important resource. While the idea that staff are important is easily accepted, the notion that you yourself might form part of the resources at your disposal often strikes a jarring chord. If you found that a member of your staff was not producing at his or her optimum, you would probably consider taking some form of action to help that person. The effective manager pays as much attention to making sure that he or she is also working at optimum level. As a manager *you* are your most important resource. If you are not performing well the organization will feel the effects. You matter and deserve attention.

Looking after yourself means looking at ways to increase your ability to cope. At the very least you need to make sure that you do not reach breaking-point. We recognize that machines break down if we do nothing to prevent it, but ignore the fact that the same fate could await us. With the variety of pressures faced and the increased pace of modern life, we seem to live our lives permanently in the fast lane. Living at top speed shortens your life. You can also damage others by not looking after yourself. When your stress is manifest then it affects the people around you. A 'blow-out' in the management team can be as destructive as a blow-out on the motorway.

In order to look after yourself you need to understand that you are a finely tuned and complex system with a finite amount of energy for coping with pressures. If you are under too much pressure for too long your system will run short of adaptive energy and will break down. At that point you will succumb to disease and illness because your system is no longer able to cope. Disease and illness are often a response to the rigours of adaptation. The timing of illness and the kind of disease you suffer are not random. They are linked to your pressure level. Many people get colds when they have been under pressure for some time — whether or not you succumb to the cold virus will be influenced by your recent experiences and the pressure you have faced. Similarly whether you succumb to more serious illness such as heart disease and cancer will depend to a large extent on whether you have been looking after yourself. You can avoid unnecessary breakdown, temporary or permanent, if you take the precaution of equipping yourself with a survival guide and following it. The first two items for your survival guide, re-evaluating situations and the skills for dealing with difficult people and situations, help you cope with some of the causes of pressure. The third item helps you be more resilient in the face of pressure.

No doctor can prescribe a medicine which will prevent breakdown. Regular medical check-ups make good sense but the important parts of your survival guide are the items *you* put into it. You have control and choice over what is in your survival guide. It is only by taking on that control and fully acknowledging the responsibility involved in looking after yourself that appropriate choices can be made.

Looking after yourself is a long-term strategy. When you meet a threat of some kind your attention is focused outwards on the danger or difficulty in front of you, not on yourself — this is not the time to think of getting yourself fitter. You need to think about preparing yourself in advance. Looking after yourself is a preventive measure.

How pressure affects your body

Before we go on to look at the steps you can take to look after yourself, you need to understand how doing so can counter the ravages of modern life. To understand this, you need to understand the autonomic nervous system.

As we have seen in earlier chapters, the fight or flight response, which helps you to respond quickly to a physical threat, can do more harm than good if it is triggered inappropriately or too frequently. The autonomic nervous system consists of two parts, the sympathetic and the parasympathetic. When the fight or flight response is triggered, the *sympathetic* side is activated. This increases your arousal level and sets in train a series of reactions which makes more energy available to you to deal with the danger.

The other side of the autonomic nervous system, the *parasympathetic,* calms you down and reduces your arousal level. When it is activated it reverses the effects of the sympathetic side. For example, your breathing and heart rate return to their previous level; blood is redistributed back to your digestive system so that the processes of digestion go on as usual; your blood pressure drops; and the cooling system returns to normal. The action of the parasympathetic side of the autonomic nervous system balances the raised level of arousal caused by the activation of the sympathetic side. The two sides of the autonomic nervous system act like a seesaw. When one side is in operation the other side is virtually dormant. What you often lose when you spend too much time under pressure is the ability — and frequently the opportunity — to activate the parasympathetic side of the autonomic nervous

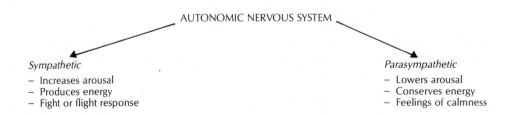

Figure 5.1 The autonomic nervous system: Control of your level of arousal

system. This leads to overuse of the sympathetic side with all its attendant physiological changes. Figure 5.1 summarizes the features of the two sides of the autonomic nervous system.

The main way in which you can get fitter for dealing with pressure is to focus on the triggering of the parasympathetic side of the autonomic nervous system. As we have seen, when you face one of your mammoths the sympathetic side of the autonomic nervous system is activated. Once the threat has passed, your level of arousal gradually decreases. However, this process takes time. If you are under pressure, long before the process is completed you will have perceived another threat. The sympathetic side is triggered again and your level of arousal increases. This is how, over time, you increase your arousal level to the maximum in incremental steps. You reach a point at which it is as though you are firing on all cylinders. If you continue at this level you will eventually become exhausted. You will wear yourself out because the soothing effects of the parasympathetic side of the autonomic nervous system have had little chance to restore the balance in your body.

Looking after yourself by exercise and relaxation

You can activate the parasympathetic side of the nervous system directly or indirectly. First we will consider how to do it directly. The two main ways available are physical exercise and relaxation techniques.

Triggering the parasympathetic directly: Physical exercise

When you are aroused you are ready for action. In the Stone Age, when people faced physical threats and the sympathetic side of the nervous system was activated, physical action followed. The physical action of running or fighting was nature's way of switching from the sympathetic to the parasympathetic side, thus restoring balance. Figure 5.2 shows how this happened.

Nowadays the chain has been broken. When you perceive a threat or danger it still leads to the triggering of the sympathetic nervous system but physical action rarely follows.

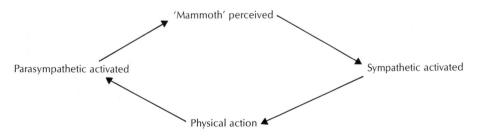

Figure 5.2 How physical action balances the two sides of the autonomic nervous system

You may be aware that when the going gets tough you feel restless and want to move about. Pacing up and down, and making trips to the coffee machine when you do not really want a drink, are examples of this. Your body is telling you what to do to restore the balance. This can pose problems at work. First, it is not always appropriate to take physical action. You often have to remain relatively still, in a meeting for example. Second, only gentle forms of exercise will normally be available to you, whereas your body has been geared up for extreme exertion. It is a good idea to move about, in whatever way you can, when you become aware that your arousal level is increasing, but you also need a long-term strategy for incorporating more vigorous exercise in your life.

Over time your body can step up its production of adrenalin. The volume of pressure constantly facing most managers means that their bodies get used to gearing up for struggles. This can lead to a vast amount of adrenalin being pumped round your system at any time. At this high level of activation a trip to the coffee machine will not be enough. It may stop the arousal level increasing any further, but will not bring your level back down to the base-line.

A long-term strategy of regular exercise will ensure that your parasympathetic side gets activated in the way most natural for your body. Regular exercise is a simple way of countering the constant activation of the sympathetic nervous system. Exercise is also beneficial in that it improves your cardiovascular functioning and muscle tone, which helps to decrease the rate of physical wear and tear.

What do we mean by exercise?

By exercise we mean physical activity. This is not to be confused with 'sport'. You can get exercise in a competitive sport but the trigger for the parasympathetic is the physical action. What we are focusing on is enjoyable exercise rather than exciting competition. Be careful not to assume that exercise and excitement must always go together.

The reason we emphasize the distinction between exercise and sporting excitement is that many managers who are not clear about it approach their exercise with the same competitive spirit that pervades their work. Many managers are concerned with winning and this can be extended to exercise as well as piloting through a new project or dealing with difficult clients. This will add to the pressures they face, not counter them. At least part of your regular exercise routine should be non-competitive. If one source of excitement in your life is a hard, competitive game of squash we are not suggesting that you cut it out but that you introduce some form of regular, rhythmic non-competitive exercise as well.

A preoccupation with winning can lead to competition against yourself even when running or swimming alone, so that non-competitive sport becomes competitive. This needs to be watched. Exercise is for your body, not another way in which you can display your talent for winning.

What kind of exercise?

Above all, when thinking about exercise as a long-term strategy for managing pressure, you need to consider what kind of exercise is enjoyable for you. If exercise becomes a chore, just another demand to be dealt with each day, then some of its beneficial effects will be undone. Everyone can find some form of exercise which they enjoy. Even walking, as long as it is brisk walking and not a gentle amble, is beneficial. It does not have to be a marathon to do you good.

It can be tempting to apply your managerial drive and determination and tackle your chosen form of exercise too vigorously. Whatever you decide to do, start gently. The two key points to bear in mind when planning to use exercise are:

- Don't overdo it.
- Enjoy it.

When considering what form of exercise is right for you it is useful to consider — apart from whether you will enjoy it — how different kinds of activity act on the body. There are three main ways in which physical activity can affect your body. It can increase your stamina, your strength or your suppleness. Let's look at *the three Ss* of physical activity in more detail.

When you improve your *stamina* you improve your heart and lung capacity and your endurance. Your body will be able to work at a higher rate for a prolonged period and will burn fuel more efficiently. Activities which improve stamina include swimming, cycling, running, jogging and brisk walking. For these activities to have their full beneficial effect they need to be sustained for at least 15 minutes.

An obvious example of a physical activity which improves your *strength* is weightlifting, but in fact most exercise incorporates an element of strength-building.

Suppleness is your body's ability to bend and be flexible. Many of the current work-out programmes are designed primarily to improve the suppleness of the body. Perhaps the most obvious example of exercises for suppleness are those which a ballet dancer does to warm up.

Although each of the three S's of exercise is important, stamina is the element which will stand you in best stead when it comes to facing pressure. You may enjoy exercise which predominantly improves strength or suppleness — such as weightlifting or a workout — but it is a good idea to ensure that you also include in your exercise routine the kind of activity which will raise your heart rate and make you sweat. The best all-round exercises for doing this are the ones we have listed for improving stamina. If you do not relish the prospect of running or cycling round the streets, you can build stamina by using exercise equipment indoors.

You need ways of improving your stamina which suit you.Not everybody is a natural runner. Although skill can be improved over time, if you find that you are not enjoying a particular activity, try something else. Not everybody takes to the same activities. Experiment until you find what is right and enjoyable for you.

The next step is to commit yourself to a regular and enjoyable routine. Finding out what exercise suits you is not going to help you until you commit yourself to doing it. To be of maximum use an exercise programme needs to be regular. Whatever your level of fitness at the start, build on it slowly but regularly. Find a pattern which suits you; do not let exercise become another pressure point.

The prospect of taking exercise may fill you with dread. You may not see yourself as a 'sporty' person, but you do not have to be 'sporty' to enjoy exercise. Exercise 5.2 will help you think through your approach to exercise. It is currently fashionable to keep fit, so kit yourself out well so that you feel good. You do not have to be the world's number one at whatever exercise you choose. You do not have to try so hard that it becomes a chore. You can ask for coaching, so that you improve and enjoy it more. You can take it slowly and surely, giving yourself space to enjoy it. You do not have to please anyone else. Exercise is for *you.*

Triggering the parasympathetic directly: Relaxation

While exercise is nature's way of triggering the parasympathetic side and ensuring a balance in the activity of your autonomic nervous system, you can also take control of your level of arousal by learning the skills of relaxation. Relaxation is an active process, not the inactive flopping into a chair which all too often marks the end of a hard day at work. Many people describe sitting slumped in front of a television, 'doing nothing', as relaxing. This so-called relaxation does not trigger the parasympathetic side of the nervous system. You can trigger the parasympathetic sitting in a chair or lying down, but it is an active technique not an inactive slump.

As with exercise, the important elements of relaxation are the breathing and the muscles. By focusing on these you can learn the techniques for triggering the parasympathetic nervous system. It is a skill, and so needs to be practised regularly. When you have developed the skill of relaxation you can use it to trigger the parasympathetic unobtrusively whenever and wherever you choose.

How we relax: The relaxation response

To demonstrate what happens when you relax, sit in a comfortable upright position and tense all your muscles as much as you can. Hold them tensed for a few seconds, then let go. What happened when you relaxed?

You probably noticed when you made yourself tense that you held your breath as well as tensing your muscles. When you let it go, you probably let your breath out as well as releasing the tension from your muscles. These are the two elements of relaxation: breathing out and pushing the tension out of your muscles.

Let's look first at breathing. As the tension mounts and the sympathetic is triggered, you breathe more quickly and more shallowly. In order to trigger the parasympathetic you need to slow down the rate of breathing and breathe deeply. You may have been told at some time in your life that if you are feeling nervous or tense it is a good idea to take a few deep breaths. This will help, but, to relax, you need to concentrate on exhaling rather than inhaling. Inhaling often reflects unease of some sort. A sigh of unhappiness, for example, is accompanied by an intake of breath, whereas a sigh of relief is usually an exhalation of air. In situations of extreme difficulty people can even stop breathing temporarily through tension, and stopping breathing can be used as a way of dealing with an intense and uncomfortable emotion. Holding yourself together by holding your breath can become a habit. To break that habit and to trigger the parasympathetic you need to focus on breathing out.

The second element of the relaxation response is easing the tension from your muscles. All too often, as people grow accustomed to living at a high level of arousal they do not notice the tension in their muscles until it becomes painful. It is very difficult to simply tell your muscles to relax. To ease the tension out of your muscles you need to emulate the cat and tense them first. The cat is a very relaxed animal but it only achieves that relaxation by stretching and tensing its muscles.

As with exercise, developing and using the skill of relaxation needs to be a long-term strategy. When used on a regular basis relaxation will improve your capacity for dealing with pressure. Relaxation not only restores the balance in your autonomic nervous system; it will also help you to sleep and aid digestion. You can learn to relax by learning specific relaxation techniques; an example is given in Ex. 5.3 at the end of the chapter. Yoga and meditation can also help you relax.

Looking after yourself by planning for balance

We have looked at two ways of directly triggering the parasympathetic side of the nervous system. In this section we are going to focus on triggering the parasympathetic indirectly. This involves planning your life in such a way that you achieve balance. You need to plan excitement and challenge in your life whilst ensuring adequate opportunity for relaxation and tranquility. In this way you can take steps to ensure that the pressure you face is right for you. Balance in your life means that there will be a match between the pressure-producing and pressure-reducing factors.

Change: Is it good for you?

Matching pressure-producing and pressure-reducing factors may seem quite straightforward in principle. However it is not always obvious which factors produce pressure and which reduce it. Events and situations which are welcome may still produce pressure. Consider your last job move. Was it something which you looked forward to? Had you been trying to get another job for a while? Was it a relief to leave your last job? Most people eagerly seek a job move, but however much you want the job and look forward to it, it will none the less require you to adapt to a new situation and this puts pressure on you. A move to a new organization, with new tasks and new people, will itself face you with demands for adaptation. The accompanying changes in your home life place even more on you. Even if the job is a promotion which you keenly sought, even if you are looking forward to the move eagerly and need the financial reward that it brings, even if it means leaving a previously intolerable job, it will still demand adaptation. *Change, whether viewed positively or negatively, is a source of pressure.*

There is an old saying that a change is as good as a rest. This is not always the case. If we change from a demanding situation to one which is comfortable, tranquil and familiar, then the change may be as good as a rest. Most organizational change means coping with an unfamiliar and probably initially uncomfortable set of circumstances. This will not be as good as a rest. For example, the reorganization of a department may involve changes in others' expectations, changes in social contacts, a change of office, a change in power structure, and changes in the tasks to be performed. However you view the change, you'll need to adjust. Your body will respond to this pressure.

To complete the picture, the level of pressure you are already experiencing at the time of the change will also influence how change affects you. If you are already under a lot of pressure, one more change can push you over into illness or exhaustion, whereas if you are below your optimum pressure level another change may act as an exciting challenge.

There are three ways of reducing the pressures of change. The first is to plan balance into your life as a whole. This means planning to spend time on the key areas of your work rather than attending to whatever lands on your desk. At the same time you need to look at your life outside work to get a balance between home and work. The second way to reduce the pressure of change is to plan time in those areas of your life which are a stable source of good feelings. The third way is to get yourself organized so that you do not rush around trying to do half a dozen things at once.

Planning your life: The macro view

Balance in your life is a vital item in your survival guide. There are two aspects of this: getting the home/work balance right and getting the balance at work right. It may well seem to you, as a busy manager, that work takes up an inordinate amount of time. Work is not, however, your whole life. What happens outside work and the amount of attention you pay to home, leisure and your social life are very important. Tempting though it may be to devote all your time to work, this is not likely to lead to effective management. It is easy, because of the pressures of work, to overlook the need to plan and nurture your home life. Taking the macro view means thinking about every area of your life, and not leaving home and leisure to chance events. They need attention in the same way as your work.

To get the balance right at work, it is crucial to keep in mind an overall view of what you are trying to achieve in your job. You need this in order to spend your time effectively. If you do not plan your time it is easy to be sidetracked by urgent but unimportant matters, and if you spend your time this way it is probable that you will experience the frustration of underachievement. You need to know in what areas of your work you actually earn the money which you are paid. It is not always obvious, nor are these areas necessarily specifically identified in your job description. Your prime responsibilities may be specific projects; sales or production targets; ensuring that reports are produced by specific deadlines; or the formulation of policy guidelines. You may also have responsibility for less tangible areas such as developing staff, maintaining departmental levels of performance or setting the tone and culture of the organization. You need to sort out what are the prime areas of your responsibility so that you ensure that you spend sufficient time and energy on these. Keeping a clear overview will enable you to say no to interesting or demanding requests which are outside your areas of prime responsibility. It will enable you to see how the day-to-day minutiae are connected to the overall purpose of your job.

Taking into account all areas of your life, you need to be aware of the sheer volume of change you are facing. Although some events by their nature bring more pressure than others, one of the main problems is the pressure brought about by cumulative changes.

The first guideline is to stagger the changes you can control. Another is to resist the temptation to counter a negative change with a positive. For example, if you are currently facing an uncertain future due to the possibility of a merger, and you are unsure of what will happen to your job, do not pick this moment to buy the house of your dreams. The positive effect of buying it will not counter the negative effects of uncertainty and job change; it will actually add to the pressures. A positive change does not counteract a negative change. Remember the effect is cumulative. Exercise 5.4 at the end of the chapter helps you to look at major change in your life.

Planning your life: The balanced view

When most of us are thinking about planning and getting better organized one major area tends to be omitted — planning time for those aspects of life which give good feelings. One of the main ways you can cope with the rapid and varied changes to which we are all subject is to pay plenty of attention to those areas of your life which act as mental havens, retreats, areas on which you can rely to provide good feelings. These areas are sometimes called 'stability zones'.

Stability zones have the opposite effect on your systems to threats. They can relate to any aspect of your life. Instead of triggering the fight or flight response, which increases your level of arousal, time in your stability zones will fill you with good feelings, and bring your arousal level down. Spending time in your stability zones is one of the most valuable ways to reduce the effects of pressure and increase your ability to cope. Yet that time has to be planned. Few people recognize the importance of stability zones, and so few people plan to spend sufficient time in them.

Six main areas in which stability zones can occur are:
- Places.
- Values and beliefs.
- Things.
- People.
- Organizations.
- Activities.

Whatever your stability zones, they will require nurturing and using if they are to help you to manage pressure.

Places — big or small, near or far

A place which provides you with comfort and the feeling of 'coming home' is an obvious example of a stability zone, as a place is an actual physical 'zone'.

A place which is a stability zone can be as large as a country. If a country and national identity provide a stability zone, then time spent abroad will feel strange. This is recognized by many organizations with staff working abroad, which provide regular trips home and education at home for children. Even when you have chosen to reside abroad, thoughts of 'home' and its customs are often a powerful source of good feelings and a sense of identity, and so can be said still to provide a stability zone.

A place which is a stability zone can also be very small, such as a particular room or even part of a room within the home — anywhere that acts as one's 'den' or personal space.

A stability zone is wherever you feel you have roots. This can be a town, often the town where the formative childhood years were spent. Or it may be a particular house. For some people the house where they grew up acts throughout the rest of life as a stability zone, even if only in memory. Places which form stability zones are not always easy to provide in our mobile society. You need to be able to adopt new ones readily or keep strong memories of comfortable places from your past.

Values and beliefs — professional, religious, political

The world of values and beliefs can give you a stable base which provides a great deal of satisfaction. Consider the professional expertise which you bring to your work; for many people this is an area central to their self-image and identity. In our society professional labels are used to define an individual, and to possess a body of knowledge and skills in a professional area is therefore an important potential stability zone.

Professional expertise and recognition are, however, only one way in which beliefs and values can act as a stability zone. Another important set of beliefs or values are those which provide a sense of meaning to life. For example, religious belief and political ideology can be very powerful in this respect. A strong belief and value system is in itself a key to increasing your ability to cope with daily pressure. It provides a framework for your daily actions, helping you make sense of what you do and what happens around you. It provides a global view of the world and a sense of perspective. Having a strong religious or political set of beliefs can counteract the tendency to view everything in purely personal terms and to see things as personally threatening.

Things — your treasured possessions

Possessions can act directly or indirectly as stability zones. Contact with a particular object can be enough to provide good feelings. For example, you can feel good simply by wearing an old, much loved item of clothing.

Possessions can act indirectly as stability zones through a connection with a happy memory. Childhood possessions or photographs often act in this way. Similarly, a particular possession — such as a certificate or a large company car — may be a stability zone because it represents an achievement or status. Cars are a common form of stability zone.

People — where you get your recognition

Managerial work by its very nature brings you into contact with a wide variety of people, and it is not uncommon to experience some degree of overload or 'people poisoning' from this intense contact with others. At times this can overshadow the fact that people can provide a very powerful source of stability and good feelings. A long, close relationship with another person can indeed be a very satisfying way of meeting some of your basic needs, such as the need for recognition and contact.

Unfortunately there are still social conventions which dictate that close relationships are acceptable in only a few circumstances. This can lead to the view that close relationships are only acceptable within the confines of a long relationship, such as marriage. While long relationships such as marriage do indeed provide stability zones for many people, the view that this is the only context where closeness and intimacy are allowed often acts to shut off other possibilities. A network of close friends and colleagues can also provide the people element of your personal stability zone map if you allow it to do so.

Organizations — where you belong

Although the work organization may most readily come to mind, any kind of organization can be a stability zone, such as a social club, sporting club, professional body or institute. The key is that you feel you belong. The occasional sense of people overload does not diminish the need for social contact, and a sense of belonging. Everyone needs this to some extent. Membership of organizations can be a powerful source of stability and good feelings.

Activities — what you do can make you feel good

The exercise of professional skills is an activity which comes readily to mind as a potential stability zone. It is useful to distinguish between, as stability zones, the possession of professional knowledge and the exercise of professional skill. For some people knowledge is the crucial element; others get their satisfaction from using skills and translating knowledge and expertise into action.

For people who get satisfaction from the exercise of professional skills, moving up the career ladder away from a professional base into a position of management can mean the loss of an important stability zone. This is often resisted by managers, who may find that their instinct is still to get involved in professional decisions rather than concentrating on their main job of managing other professionals. However, exercise of managerial skills can itself become a new stability zone, with the attendant good feelings.

Hobbies are another source of stability zones, whether the activity involved is done in isolation and is of itself a source of good feelings, or whether it involves association with others and provides a stability zone on this basis. Everyone needs stability zones, but not everyone needs the same ones. The key is to be clear what aspects of your life act in this way and to plan to spend time on them.

Because your stability zones are so important, any threat to them can provide you with some of your worst moments. It makes sense to ensure that you have a range of stability zones so that if one is threatened you still have others to rely on. The same stability zones may not be available to you all your life. Change is a fact of life. You will retire one day; you may face redundancy; your friends may move away or die. You need to plan new ways of getting good feelings and satisfactions. If, for example, one of your stability zones has been a strenuous sport and it is becoming less enjoyable as you are getting older, you may need to consider stopping that activity and taking up a less energetic sport, or you may choose a completely different aspect of your life to rely on to provide satisfaction.

To use your stability zones to the full, you need to recognize that they are an important part of your survival guide and that it is sensible, not self-indulgent, to nurture them. Once you have recognized that, the guidelines in Table 5.2 and Ex. 5.5 at the end of the chapter will help you make the best use of them.

- Identify them.
- Plan to use them.
- Ensure you have a range of them.
- Foster them.
- Plan replacements.

Table 5.2 Guidance for ensuring that stability zones are always in your survival guide

Planning your life: The micro view

Once you have gained an overview of your life and how you want to spend your time, and planned the use of your stability zones, there is one remaining area which will reward attention — the day-to-day management of your life. This means planning your diary sensibly. There is no point planning to spend time on an important stability zone during a weekend a couple of months away if, through lack of organization, you run yourself into the ground before then. A simple example of what we mean is planning to go down to London for a morning meeting, to Bath for an afternoon meeting and to Birmingham for an evening meeting. Many managers we speak to delegate the detailed organization of their diary to people who do not always understand the pressures of constant travel. Explaining what you want to the people who actually organize your time will help eradicate this difficulty. In the same way you can get into difficulties by planning an important social event on the same day as an important, long management team meeting. These may seem simple problems to avoid but they crop up repeatedly unless you actually organize a system for dealing with them.

You cannot plan every moment of your day. Unscheduled events and crises are inevitable. None the less, you need to make sure that your day has a sensible pattern. Plan time for exercise, relaxation and your stability zones on a day-to-day basis. Exercise 5.6 helps you think through your priorities and how to plan your day-to-day life in accordance with them.

The don'ts: Dangerous habits

Much of this chapter has been about learning the habits of a healthy lifestyle. Most of us have bad habits to unlearn as well — dangerous but common 'props' which don't really work to reduce stress even if we have the impression that they do. Unhealthy habits are often acquired as a way of coping with too much or too little pressure; they offer some short-term satisfaction and comfort and so make people feel better for a while. They can then develop into dangerous habits which are used whether a person is under pressure or not. The more common dangerous props are cigarettes, tranquillizers, alcohol, coffee, junk food and sweets. With the exception of cigarettes these may do little harm in moderation. The problem is that, used as props, consumption tends to increase to levels which are unacceptable for a healthy body.

Tobacco

Many people smoke to help them relax, or as a way of punctuating a stressful situation. The ritual of lighting up a cigarette, the pleasure of exhaling smoke, as well as the physiological satisfaction of nicotine dependency, all contribute to a powerful habit which is not easy to break. The immediate satisfaction is often more compelling than the knowledge that smoking can damage your health. However strong that satisfaction, it is a myth that smoking helps you cope with stress; in the long term it creates it. Your body has one more problem to cope with, as the smoke you inhale is a very dangerous invader. Breathing and relaxation exercises are far more effective ways of coping with pressure. Nicotine dependency is as much a drug dependency as addiction to heroin. Smoking does nothing to help you cope with the underlying causes of pressure in your life.

Tranquillizers and sleeping pills

You may be prescribed tranquillizers or sleeping pills by your doctor if you are under considerable pressure. They can help you to cope with distress for a short period of time. However it is very easy to become dependent on tranquillizers if you use them for a prolonged period. They lose their medical potency if you continue to take them for more than a few weeks or so, but by then you may be getting addicted. If this happens you may experience severe withdrawal symptoms when you stop taking them. Doctors vary in their approach to prescribing tranquillizers; some are more sensitive than others to their abuse. If you do need tranquillizers as a short-term aid to coping, do ensure that you discuss the effects of the particular drug with your doctor.

Alcohol

Abuse of alcohol is now being recognized as a serious problem. Many people argue that a little alcohol aids digestion, but the effects of alcohol dependency are very dangerous. It may seem that the rigours of a hard day can be eased away by a pre-dinner drink, but alcohol is not a relaxant, as many people believe; rather it depresses the activity of certain parts of the brain. In psychological terms it first of all inhibits your ability to make judgements and distorts your sense of priorities, and thus you will feel good because you stop reminding yourself of all your responsibilities. At the next level of consumption it interferes with your ability to deal with current reality. Eventually it depresses your brain's control over your body. Alcohol does not trigger the parasympathetic nervous system, and so does not help you cope with stressful situations; and like the other drugs we have talked about it does nothing to tackle the underlying sources of pressure you face. Heavy abuse of your body with alcohol at best creates an extra physical demand for your body to adapt to; at worst it changes your behaviour, damages your health and disrupts your capacity to cope effectively.

Coffee

Coffee is a prime source of caffeine. The odd cup of coffee will not do long-term damage to your system, but continuous drinking through the working day will. Amongst other effects caffeine affects your heart rate. It acts as a stimulant, increasing the rate at which your heart beats. Being fit to cope with pressure means reducing our levels of arousal, including our resting heart rate. Caffeine is counter-productive in this and can produce long-term effects. One of the most noticeable behavioural effects for many people is disrupted sleeping patterns. Caffeine is also an ingredient of tea and cola drinks, which are thus no more helpful as props than coffee.

Junk food and sweets

Unlike the other props we have listed, these are not drugs. In themselves they are not harmful, but they become so if eaten instead of a properly balanced diet. Many people turn to junk food and sweets when under pressure, because such foods are associated with a feeling of comfort; indeed they are often called 'comfort foods'. They usually offer food in a form which fills you up or gives you a quick injection of sugar. Many people feel a need for oral satisfaction when the world seems threatening, but getting comfort in this way can create problems. Apart from the fact that junk foods and sweets may come to replace more nutritious foods in your diet, if you eat too many calories you may put on more weight than you want, and this can be an additional source of pressure.

Balance in your diet: A safe and useful prop for your body

Junk food and sweets typify an unbalanced diet. A diet high in junk foods is likely to contain too much sugar (a 'hidden' constituent of many convenience foods), too much salt (which is added to most processed food), too much fat (from fried food and other sources) and too little fibre. There is no single pattern of food intake which suits everyone. You need to be aware of how you feel after eating different kinds of food and choose a diet which suits you. You probably know when you are eating badly. However there are some simple themes running through the advice on healthy eating: most of us consume too much salt, sugar and fat, and too little roughage or fibre. The difficulty for most people in changing this is twofold: first, it necessitates an awareness of what foods contain; and second, you need to plan your eating. For example, a common lunch at work is a cheese sandwich made from white bread, and a bar of chocolate. This is a high-sugar, high-fat, low-fibre meal. If this is the only food easily available to you at lunchtime, avoiding it will involve planning, and when you are under a lot of pressure it is easy to forget to plan what you eat. Unbalanced diets are associated with many of the serious stress illnesses — for instance, heart disease and certain cancers, such as cancer of the colon. It makes sense to put a healthy diet on the list of items in your survival guide.

Survival guides: A long-term view

The survival guide items we have discussed in this chapter are all open to abuse. If you make a martyr of yourself by slavishly following an exercise routine you hate or doing relaxation exercises in every spare minute; if you make a chore of planning your life, choose boring stability zones, or suddenly become teetotal and restrict your diet so that no 'goodies' are included; you are in danger of keeping it up for a week but then going back to old habits. You need to choose items which suit you, and which above all you can enjoy.

Exercises for Chapter 5: Getting fitter to deal with pressure

Exercise 5.1 How easy do you find it to look after yourself?

It is not always easy to devote effort to looking after ourselves because we all carry around a set of values and beliefs which tell us that this is wrong. Read through the following statements and mark whether you agree or disagree with each one.

agree/disagree

1. It is always better to spend my time on others rather than on myself.
2. Looking after myself is sensible.
3. What I want or need for myself is less important than what other people want from me.
4. I am important and my needs are important.
5. Looking after myself is selfish.
6. I deserve attention from myself.
7. I am not worth spending time on and looking after.
8. I must look after myself because only then am I in a fit state to look after other people, if I choose to.
9. No grown person should need looking after; only children need looking after.
10. Other people matter but so do I.
11. Other people matter more than I do.
12. Everybody needs looking after, whatever their age.
13. If I do require some care and attention I will have to fight for it.
14. If I need some care and attention, it is up to me to be assertive in asking for what I need.

Scoring

Score 3 for each time you agreed with an even-numbered item. Score 3 for each time you disagreed with an odd-numbered item.

The maximum score is 42. If you scored *between 30 and 42* you have a set of values and beliefs which will help you in taking care of yourself. You are unlikely to have much difficulty developing a strategy to look after yourself.

If you scored *between 21 and 30* you have some views which could get in the way of your care of yourself. You may need to re-evaluate these before you can plan an effective strategy.

If you scored *less than 21* it is likely that you will find it hard to plan a programme for looking after yourself, because your attitudes do not predispose you to take care of yourself. The values and beliefs you hold will get in the way of devising a constructive survival pack. You will help yourself if you can develop a more positive view of the need to take care of yourself.

Exercise 5.2 *What are your views about exercise?*

A regular programme of exercise is one of the most useful ways of getting fitter to cope with pressure. How easy you will find it to incorporate exercise into your survival pack will depend on how you view it. Read through the following statements and mark whether you agree or disagree with each one.

1. Exercise is fun for me.   *agree/disagree*
2. Exercise is only fun for me if it is competitive.
3. Exercise is enjoyable for me.
4. Exercise is hard work for me.
5. Exercise is good for me.
6. Exercise is an effort for me.
7. Exercise leads to good feelings for me.
8. Exercise is boring for me.
9. Exercise is something I look forward to.
10. Exercise is difficult for me.

Scoring

Score 3 for each time you agreed with an odd-numbered item. Score 3 for each time you disagreed with an even-numbered item.

The maximum score is 30. If you scored *21 or above* you will not find it too difficult to use exercise as part of your survival pack. You seem to view exercise in a positive light and probably exercise already. You may want to review your current exercise pattern to ensure that it is regular enough to maintain your fitness.

If you scored *between 12 and 20* you will not find it so easy to incorporate an exercise element into your survival pack as you do not view it as particularly enjoyable. You probably recognize its beneficial effects and need to experiment to find something which you enjoy and which perhaps has a social aspect so that your motivation can be more easily maintained.

If you scored *less than 11* you probably dislike exercise; perhaps even the idea of it is an anathema. Your difficulty may be that you have become so set against exercise that you are in danger of actively finding ways of avoiding it! Experiment with things that have even a little appeal, until you feel more at ease with it.

Exercise 5.3 Learning to relax

This exercise covers in simple stages the process of relaxation by which you can activate your parasympathetic nervous system. Early in the instructions we ask you to close your eyes, so it is a good idea to read through all the stages before practising it! Even better, get someone else to read the instructions to you. An alternative is to record the instructions on to a tape, which you can then play through whenever you practise. As your skill develops you will no longer need the tape, but it can be helpful in the early stages. Remember to take time over each stage, you cannot relax in a hurry!

1. Find a comfortable position

Find a position in which you are sitting or lying comfortably — in an easy chair or on the floor or a bed. Sitting upright will not be an easy position in which to relax as so many of your muscles are involved in maintaining the position. If you are lying down you might like to put a small cushion or pillow under your head and under your knees; most people find this makes this position very comfortable. Close your eyes.

2. Focus on your breathing

Place one hand on your stomach, just below your rib cage. Breathe in through your nose, pushing air to the bottom of your lungs so that your hand is pushed outwards. Concentrate on filling your lungs right to the bottom and expanding them. Hold for a few seconds.... Now slowly push the air out through your mouth. Make a conscious effort to expel all the air. Repeat this a few times until you are comfortable breathing in deeply, expanding your lungs and slowly exhaling.

3. Focus on your muscles

In this section we will be asking you to tighten groups of muscles. When you follow the instruction to tighten your muscles do not tighten them so hard that you cramp them.

Place your hands on your lap or at your side, whichever is most comfortable.

- Now concentrate on your feet. Tighten the muscles in your feet as hard as you can and hold them tense for a few seconds. Now let go. Again, tighten the muscles in your feet as hard as you can, hold for a few seconds, then let go.
- Now concentrate on your lower legs. Tighten your calf muscles as hard as you can, squeeze them tightly and hold the tension for a few seconds. Now let it go. Again, tighten your lower legs as hard as you can, hold for a few seconds, then let go.

- Now concentrate on your thigh muscles. Tighten your thigh muscles as hard as you can, and hold for a few seconds. Now let go. Again, tighten your thigh muscles as hard as you can, hold, then let go.
- Now concentrate on your buttocks. Tighten your buttock muscles as hard as you can, and hold for a few seconds. Now let go. Again, tighten your buttock muscles as hard as you can, hold, then let go.
- Now your stomach; tighten your stomach muscles as hard as you can, really tense them and hold for a few seconds. Now let go. Again, tighten your stomach muscles as hard as you can, hold, then let go.
- Now concentrate on your hands. Clench your fists into a ball and tighten them as hard as you can, and hold for a few seconds. Now let go. Again, clench your fists as hard as you can, hold, then let go.
- Now your shoulders; tighten your shoulders as much as you can, really hunch them up, and hold for a few seconds. Now let go. Again, tighten your shoulders as hard as you can, hold, then let go.
- Now your jaw; clench your teeth and tense your jaw as hard as you can. Really tighten your jaw, and hold for a few seconds. Now let go. Again, tighten your jaw as hard as you can, hold, then let go.
- Finally, concentrate on your forehead and eyes. Screw your eyes tightly shut and frown as hard as you can, and hold for a few seconds. Now let go. Again, screw your eyes shut and frown as hard as you can, hold, then let go.
- Now concentrate on each group of muscles in turn. If you can feel any tension left in any part of you, ease it out by tightening the muscle and then letting it go. Do this until you have eased out all the tension and the muscle feels relaxed.
- Stay in the same position and focus on your breathing again. There is no need to put your hand on your stomach this time; simply breathe in deeply right down to the bottom of your lungs and slowly exhale. Repeat a few times.

4. Sit up

When you feel relaxed and tranquil, gently open your eyes and slowly sit up.

5. How do you feel?

Keep still for a few minutes and become aware of how you feel. Congratulations! You have just triggered the parasympathetic part of your nervous system directly.

6. Planning to relax

Relaxing, like any skill, needs practice. When you have developed the skill you will be able to reduce your arousal level on demand when you face mammoths or anticipate doing so. However you will continue to benefit from regular 15–20 minute relaxation sessions. In this way you can build balance into the activity of your autonomic nervous system.

Plan regular short sessions of relaxation, whenever and wherever suits you. Last thing at night is often a good time, as the relaxation will trigger the parasympathetic ready for a good night's sleep. You will get benefit from three or four sessions a week, but to make the most of the technique you need more frequent sessions.

Exercise 5.4 Changes in your life

How fit you are to cope with pressure will depend to a large extent on what has been happening in your life recently. Reflect on the last year and note down the changes that have occurred in each area of your life. Then reflect on what you predict will happen during the next year.

Changes at work

What changes occured in your working life? (E.g., moving jobs, transferring to another type of work, changing offices, retiring, redundancy, experiencing a merger, joining a new team.)

What has happened in the last year	*What I predict will happen in the next year*

Changes in domestic life

What changes have there been in your domestic life? (E.g., a change in residence, additions or losses in membership of your household, changes in the nature of close domestic relationships, someone in the house suffering an illness.)

What has happened in the last year	*What I predict will happen in the next year*

Changes in social life

What changes have there been in your social life? (E.g., changes in club membership, new friends, loss of friends through moving or death, changes in the nature of your social network.)

What has happened in the last year	What I predict will happen in the next year

Other changes

Are there any other changes which have affected you personally? (E.g., trouble with the law, change in financial standing, sexual difficulties, taking a holiday, changing diet.)

What has happened in the last year	What I predict will happen in the next year

Changes in the past year: The overview

Thinking of all the changes you have experienced in your life over the past year will give you a clearer idea of the amount of adaptation you have been experiencing.

yes/no

Have there been changes in more than one area?
Have the changes involved major upheaval?
Is the cumulative effect of change in your life high at the moment?

If cumulative change is high, have you noticed any effects of this — in your behaviour, your feelings, your thinking or your physical health?

Changes you predict for the next year: The overview

Reflecting on the changes you predict for the next year will give you a clearer idea of the amount of adjusting you will have to do.

yes/no

Will there be changes in more than one area?
Will the changes involve major upheaval?
Will the cumulative effect of change be high next year?

If you expect a great deal of change to accumulate next year you will need to pay special attention to making time and space to slow down and relax if you intend to stay fit and healthy. You will need to counterbalance the affects of this pressure.

You may be able to avoid some of the changes or postpone them. What actions are you willing to take?

Exercise 5.5   Stability zones: Sources of good feelings

It is important to have stability zones in your life, as without them it is easy to succumb to pressure. Stability zones are areas of your life which act as mental havens, retreats and sources of good feelings. You need to be able to rely on them. Use this exercise to think about what your stability zones are and what you would like them to be.

What are your stability zones?

What *values and beliefs* do you hold which provide you with a secure base?

What *places,* large or small, provide you with roots or security?

Who are the *people* in your life whom you can rely on and who act as stability zones for you?

What *organizations* do you belong to which provide you with a sense of belonging and good feelings?

What *activities* do you do which act as stability zones and anchors in your life?

Do you need to change the pattern of your stability zones?

Are there any changes you would like to make in your stability zone pattern? For example, do you have enough, are they reliable, and will they serve you in the future?

If you have identified any changes you would like to make, how are you going to implement those changes?

Exercise 5.6 *Planning for pressure at work*

Focus on your working life. To have a sense of direction and plan accordingly you need to be clear about the prime responsibilities of your job.

1. What are the prime responsibilties of your work as you see them? (Confine yourself to about half a dozen prime areas.)

2. What do you think are the prime responsibilities of your work as your staff sees them?

3. What do you think are the prime responsibilities of your work as your boss sees them?

4. Are you clear in your responses to 1, 2 and 3? If not, what can you do to get a clear view of your prime responsibilities?

5. Are there any discrepancies between your answers to 1, 2 and 3? If so, what can you do to resolve those differences?

Now you have identified your prime areas of responsibility at work you need to plan your day-to-day activities to fit in with these. It is very easy to have a mismatch between long-term goals, prime areas of responsibility and what you actually spend your time *doing*.

There are now many systems on the market for helping you organize your time according to your priorities and you may find one of these helpful. However, even if you don't choose to buy a commercial system, you can still improve your diary planning.

Making time for your prime areas of responsibility: What am I doing?

Look through your diary for the last month to get an impression of how you spend your time now. How much time did you spend on each of your prime areas of responsibility? Was it sufficient? What didn't you do that you need to plan for?

Prime area of responsibility	Time spent	Sufficient time yes/no	Tasks uncompleted
1.			
2.			
3.			
4.			
5.			
6.			
7.			

Making time for your prime areas of responsibility: What should I be doing?

Now start planning for the future. Begin by looking through your prime areas of responsibility; list the main tasks that you need to do in each.

Area 1

Tasks:

Area 2

Tasks:

Area 3

Tasks:

Area 4

Tasks:

Area 5

Tasks:

Area 6

Tasks:

Pick a suitable planning period for the kind of job you do. This will depend on the timescale of the operations you manage and the length of the dominant cycle in your work. For example, a head teacher might choose an academic year; a production manager might choose a month's cycle; a sales manager might choose the next period over which sales targets are measured.

For the set of tasks associated with each prime area, map out the amount of time you need for each task and the timing of it in the period you have chosen. Decide who else will be involved in working on the task. Make a *task plan*.

Book time in your diary for these tasks *even when you will be working alone;* treat these times as fixed appointments and fit other meetings around them. If necessary, to make space for yourself which is uninterrupted, book a conference room or somewhere else where you can think and write without being disturbed, just as you would for a meeting with others.

Thinking strategically

An important feature of day-to-day planning is keeping two levels of thinking going at the same time: an overall view of where you are going, and a very detailed decision process about how to spend your time from hour to hour. To remind you, paste a copy of this prompter in the front of your diary and keep referring to it.

Where am I aiming to go?
What do I need to do to get there?
Why I am doing this at the moment?
How can I avoid wasting time right now?
Whom should I be spending my time with now?
When is that important task going to be done?

Part 2

The manager's guide to organizational survival

In this part of the book we turn our attention to managing pressure in the organization. In Part 1 we focused on managing your own pressure levels because you are the most important resource for which you are responsible as a manager. Only when you have developed the skills of coping with pressure at work and feel fit to survive modern organizational life are you ready to turn your attention to your second most important resource — the people you manage.

We are focusing now on the need to recognize when inappropriate pressure exists in the organization and how you as a manager can create an organizational survival guide. The process is similar to the one you went through in Part 1 but the focus has changed. In order to design a suitable organizational survival guide, you need to identify what kind of stress is evident in the organization. We start with this in Chapter 6. We will then look at three ways in which you can create your organizational survival guide: first by enhancing the helping skills you need for dealing with people who are stressed (Chapter 7); then by taking steps to prevent stress occurring in the organization (Chapter 8); and finally by considering ways of making the organization fitter to deal with pressure (Chapter 9).

6. Recognizing stress in others: Are there mammoths in the office?

In this chapter we shall focus on recognizing stress in others. You need to do this in order to:

- Know whether and where stress is occurring in your organization.
- Assess whether the roots of stress lie in the organization.
- Develop an organizational survival guide which can tackle organizational stress in your area of operation.

Organizational stress is any stress which is apparent when people are at work. It is not always caused by events at work, as you will see when we examine the 'stress chain reaction'. However, many symptoms of stress can be alleviated by the actions taken by you as a manager.

Why organizational stress is a problem

Each person needs an optimum level of pressure in order to perform well, and so do organizations. When individuals move away from their optimum pressure level, not only do they become uncomfortable but their performance is affected. The same applies to an organization. When the pressure falls too low an organization becomes stodgy and sleepy, and will not fully energize its resources. At the other extreme, if the pressure level is too high, the organization will struggle and become tense, which will hinder effective and efficient performance. A slight shift in pressure level around the optimum will not necessarily result in stress; it is more likely to result in feelings of discomfort or provide the impetus for needed change, adaptation and innovation. As with individuals, it is at the extremes that pressure causes problems.

The stress chain reaction

One of the problems facing you as you scan the organization for signs of stress is that it is not always easy to distinguish between cause and effect. Your skill as an observer of stress in the organization will be helped if you take into account the 'stress chain reaction' — the process by which stress in one part of the social system puts pressure on the other parts. This is shown in Fig. 6.1. Although we

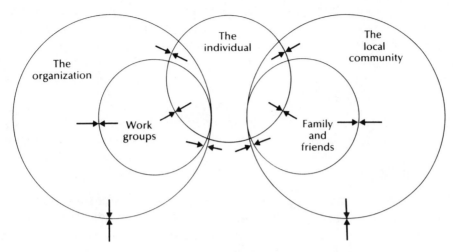

Society – economy, politics, cultural and social expectations

Figure 6.1 The stress chain reaction: How stress is transmitted through the social system

focus in this book on the organization, people live within a broader context, and pressure they experience at home can be brought to work, and similarly stress experienced because of work can be carried outside. When we are looking at the stress manifested in the organization, we must take into account the fact that some pieces in our information base will be missing. As a manager you mainly have access to the organization system, and stress symptoms exhibited outside the organization may not come to your attention. Also, stress may be caused by pressures outside the organization which are unknown to you, and so stress brought to work from outside can be difficult to diagnose. Your responsibility as a manager is to observe whatever you can within the organization and to do what you can within the organizational boundary. You cannot influence every part of the social system.

An individual experiencing stress puts pressure on the section or team, as well as on the organization. A group experiencing stress puts pressure on individual members as well as the wider organization. An organization experiencing stress puts pressure on individuals and working groups. Pressure is transmitted between the three levels of an organization in a number of ways.

For example, if an individual is stressed and is away from work with a stress-related illness, this places extra demands on the remaining members of the work team. Even if the stressed person stays at work his or her ability to do the job may well be affected, either through changes in his or her ability to think and make decisions, or because emotional changes are hindering performance. This will also affect the work of the team. A stressed person can also put pressure on the organization; by using the welfare or medical services, for example, or by engaging in forms of industrial action.

Similarly, if a departmental management team is facing intense pressure with which it is unable to cope, its meetings may become disorganized and its discussion irrelevant, and this will be an uncomfortable experience for its members because it will affect their ability to get on with their own work. It will also affect the overall management of the organization, because the necessary decisions may not be taken.

A stressed organization may, for example, respond to excessive demands by denying them and avoiding making strategic decisions. This will pose problems for the groups who work within the overall strategic framework. It will also cause problems for individuals if key policy decisions are not made.

The picture is further complicated by the fact that signs of stress can result from a stress chain reaction within each part of the organization, as well as between parts. For example, stress in the organization as a whole may be demonstrated by a high rate of staff turnover which in turn will place pressure on the organization because of the influx of new and possibly inexperienced staff. A working group may manifest stress through lengthy and unproductive meetings, for example, which in turn puts pressure on the group as it becomes less likely that its objectives will be achieved in the time available. At the individual level, stress may be manifested by people drinking more at lunch-time, for example, which in turn exerts pressure as it becomes more difficult for them to maintain performance in the afternoon.

Symptoms of stress can accumulate as the chain reaction lengthens. For example, drinking at lunch-time may lead to mistakes being made, which may lead to a missed deadline, which may lead to a row, which may lead to more drinking the following lunch-time, and so on. In this case there will be several indications that stress is present. It may not be easy to piece together all the links in the chain, but the starting-point is alertness to signs that stress is present. The drinking at lunch-time, the missed deadline, the mistakes in work or the row are all signs that there may well be stress in the organization.

Your role as a manager in recognizing and dealing with pressure

Let us now consider your role in recognizing and managing pressure. You may think that you already have enough to do without being worried about the pressure other people face. We have frequently encountered the response that it is just one more item to add to the list of things a manager has to find time for. Time is a precious and finite resource and it can be difficult to fit in all that you need to do. Managing pressure in others does take time, but in view of the consequences of not doing so it is time well spent. We have also heard the view that it is not a manager's job to act as a 'therapist' to staff. We are not suggesting that managers become therapists, but are presenting strategies and skills you can use as a manager to recognize when stress is present in the organization, so that you can develop an organizational survival guide which prevents the consequences of inappropriate and prolonged pressure.

As a manager you are responsible for the work of other people. If your section or department is not achieving its targets you are held accountable. It is your responsibility to take steps to ensure that your staff are performing at their best. This role is crucial in ensuring that the organization performs well.

Some managers take the view that the pressure experienced by staff is nothing to do with them. They argue that members of staff who cannot cope with the situations that arise should leave. This is the view that if you can't stand the heat, you should get out of the kitchen; that the stress experienced by staff is their own problem. There is a grain of truth in this; people are responsible for their own actions and behaviour but this does not mean that it is nothing to do with their manager. Reactions and feelings in so far as they affect performance are very much a managerial concern.

Stress in the organization: What to look for

The first step in managing pressure in the organization is to recognize when people are moving away from their optimum pressure level and stress is a problem.

Stress in the organization can be identified at three levels: the person, the group and the organization. Recognizing stress depends on your skills of observation, which in turn depend on knowing what to look for, understanding the stress chain reaction, and preventing unconstructive attitudes from distorting perception.

The key is the match between the pressures faced by the organization, group or individual and their abilities to cope. A mismatch at any level results in stress. You are looking for signs of movement away from optimum pressure level. You are looking for change.

What to look for when observing individuals

The presence of stress in an individual can be observed in four main areas — the mental, the physical, the emotional and the behavioural. When you were considering your own responses to inappropriate pressure you were able to examine all four areas, but you do not have direct access to the physical experience, feelings or thoughts of others. You can only gather evidence about these indirectly through behaviour.

Behaviour can be thought of as having two aspects: *what* we say and do, and *how* we say and do it. It is easy to concentrate on the former to the exclusion of the latter but both are important when looking for signs of stress in others.

People may tell you directly that they are stressed but more frequently they will give indications through their behaviour. Table 6.1 shows the main areas to observe when looking for signs of stress in others.

	What	How
Behaviour	Unusual behaviour Misplaced behaviour	Gestures Facial expression Degree of eye contact
Speech	Topics raised Choice of words	Tone of voice Pitch and inflection Degree of fluency

Table 6.1 Signs of stress in other people

Stress may be apparent in the topics raised in conversation, and the specific words used. If a person keeps going back to a topic, for example, this may well be an indication that he or she is worried about it. The use of words with strong emotional overtones — words like 'terrible', 'disastrous' or 'horrendous' — may indicate that the speaker has strong underlying feelings. Unusual or misplaced behaviour is a third source of information. Unusual behaviour is behaviour you would not expect from a particular person. We often say that people are 'not themselves' or that something is 'not like' them when we notice them behaving in a way which is unusual for them. It may be that they are behaving in a completely new way, or it may be a question of an increase or decrease in customary behaviour. An example of someone behaving in a new way might be someone staying quiet all through a management team meeting, when normally he or she is a lively contributor. An example of an increase in customary behaviour is a member of staff coming to you for assistance more frequently than you would expect knowing the tasks he or she is working on. You also need to be alert to misplaced behaviour — behaviour which is inappropriate for the setting. An example of this might be someone picking an argument in public about a topic best left for private discussion.

How someone speaks or acts is also vital evidence when you are looking for signs of stress. With speech, the tone of voice used, the degree of fluency and the pitch and inflection of the voice tell us a great deal about how someone is feeling. With actions, the gestures used, posture, facial expressions, degree of eye contact, and distance from other people provide valuable information. For example, if a member of staff who normally uses relaxed and open gestures begins to appear tense around the shoulders, stops making eye contact with people, has an immobile expression and clenches his or her fist during meetings, you are being given important information about his or her current experience. There is no single or universal pattern of behaviour which indicates stress. You need to be alert to behaviours which are misplaced or unusual for a particular person.

When you are looking at patterns of behaviour in other people you are looking for change. It can sometimes be change in specific behaviours, but not infrequently there will be a change in the general level of activity exhibited. An example of this is someone pacing up and down. As we have seen, the body's way of coping with pressure is to trigger the fight or flight response, gearing itself up for strenuous physical action. Many of the changes in behaviour you will notice are the observable elements of the fight or flight response, and it is helpful to keep this in mind when watching for signs of stress in other people.

It is possible to recognize signs of the fight or flight reaction even when you are meeting someone for the first time and you have no way of knowing whether the behaviour is unusual for them. Fast or shallow breathing, perspiration and muscle tension may all be signs that the fight or flight reaction has been activated. It is easier to detect signs of stress in other people — whether or not you know them well — when you are skilled at observing behaviour. Exercise 6.1 at the end of the chapter will set you on the path to recognizing stress amongst the individuals on your staff.

What to look for when observing groups or teams

As a manager, you are responsible for ensuring that teams work well, so you'll need to recognize any stress present in the groups you manage. There are two ways in which to gain information about the pressure level of a group or team. The first is observation of the behaviour within the group during meetings. The second is observation of behaviour outside group meetings: what the members say about the group, and how they refer to it; and how the group relates to other groups.

A work group is more than the sum of the individual members. If a member of a group appears stressed, it may not be solely a personal problem. It may be that, because of the way the team operates, one individual is acting as the 'scapegoat' and bearing the pressure for the whole group. Close observation of the group will indicate whether or not the whole group is stressed.

Close observation of a group entails being alert to two aspects of group working: how people in the group relate to each other; and how they get the work done. Observing how a group performs its tasks involves noting the content of discussion; the method by which the agenda is determined and the minutes are recorded; and the procedures adopted for managing discussions. Observing how group members relate to each other is often more difficult, because relationships are less overt than procedures. Relationships in the group can be observed in behaviours which show the patterns of power plays, likes and dislikes between people, alliances and coalitions, unspoken agendas, communications within the group, conflict and the way it is handled, and the level of harmony and cohesiveness. You need to observe both how the group works and the relationships within it to understand what is happening in a group so that you can detect signs of stress, but it is often the relationships which are the better source of information.

The relationships between members of a working group or team will be affected by the pressure experienced by the group. In particular, as relationships deteriorate you will be able to observe behaviours which are group equivalents of the fight or flight response in an individual. These give you a clue that a group is in a tight spot. When a group is threatened, energy and attention will be geared to survival rather than performance and achievement.

Fight	Flight
– People spend time during group discussion on retaliation.	– Few people contribute to discussions.
– Mistakes used to punish people.	– Group members work in isolation, not as a group.
– Unhealthy competition.	– No sharing of common problems.
– Psychological games and 'politicking'.	– No progress review or attention given to how the group is working.
– High level of aggressive behaviour.	– High level of unassertion, leaving leader to make decisions.

Table 6.2 Fight or flight behaviour in working groups: Symptoms of group stress

Table 6.2 shows some examples of fight or flight behaviour which can be observed in stressed groups. When behaviours such as these are exhibited in a working group there will be a low level of trust between group members; lack of creativity in problem solving, and of honesty and directness; a low level of assertive behaviour; poor attention to the development of group members; and general feelings of dissatisfaction (which will often be attributed to the formal leadership, whether or not this is the actual cause of the problem). All are signs of a stressed group.

When a group is struggling with too much pressure two things tend to happen. First, the group is likely to see difficulties wherever it looks, because of its high state of arousal. Second, despite internal conflicts, group members often cling together in the face of perceived threat from outsiders. Often other groups within the organization are perceived as threatening, which leads to a deterioration of relationships with other groups. Becoming skilled and practised at observing what is happening within a group will help you to detect signs of a stressed group. Exercise 6.2 helps you do this.

What to look for when taking an overview of your organization or department

As a manager you have overall responsibility for a part of the organization. Symptoms of stress can be observed at the organizational or departmental level as well as in individuals and groups. Here the focus is shifted to information about patterns of behaviour within the organization. When the whole organization is under too much pressure, patterns of stress symptoms on a large scale can be observed. The skill of monitoring an organization or department for stress involves the collection of information on a systematic basis across the organization, and for this you need to know what to look for.

Some stress responses at the organizational level are easily monitored and lend themselves to observation and quantifiable measurement. Others do not lend themselves to quantifiable measurement, but none the less can be observed — these are the hidden symptoms of organizational stress. Whether they are easily measurable or hidden, organizational symptoms of stress, like those in the individual and the group, can be related to the fight or flight response. Many of the indicators of organizational stress can be seen as individual reactions, until the pattern emerges and you become aware that the symptom is not an isolated occurrence but widespread. One person off sick regularly will not necessarily reflect stress within the whole department, but if a high proportion of staff are away regularly, a problem at the organizational level is indicated. We are now looking out for large-scale patterns of fighting or fleeing. Table 6.3 gives some examples of behaviour which are organizational indicators of fight or flight, and further examples include a high accident rate, poor decision making, poor quality and quantity of work, low morale, and general dissatisfaction.

	Quantitative indicators	*Qualitative indicators*
Fight	Strikes Downtime Sabotage Grievances	Poor relationships: – animosity – distrust – disrespect
Flight	Absenteeism Lateness High staff turnover High sickness rates	Low level of effort Low level of interpersonal contact

Table 6.3 Organizational fight or flight: Symptoms of organizational stress

These signs of stress are cause for concern in themselves, but two further steps are necessary to give a clearer indication of an inappropriate pressure level in the organization. The first is to note whether there is a change in the rate or level of the activity you are monitoring; the second is to use comparative information from other organizations or departments. For example, a high rate of absenteeism in a department compared with a year ago could reflect a changing level of pressure which has become inappropriate. A high level in any of these indicators when compared with similar organizations or departments may indicate the same thing.

When making such comparisons you need to think carefully about what should be compared with what. There is little point in assessing change between the position today and that of ten years ago; it is a comparison over months, or at most a year or two, which gives the best information. If you are making comparisons between organizations, either in whole or part, you must compare like with like and the two should be equivalent in terms of size, skills, type of work, and the profile of the workforce. Comparing British Rail with a private architect's practice is not a sensible exercise.

Identifying stress at the organizational level depends not so much on your personal skills of observation as on your skill in establishing monitoring systems to provide you with the information you need. It is difficult to make useful observations about aggregated patterns such as sickness rate or staff turnover in other than an intuitive or impressionistic sense unless records are kept. It is premature to decide on a suitable period of time for assessing change or on a comparable organization or department if the data for a comparison are not available.

Exercise 6.3 looks at the recognition of stress at the organizational or departmental level.

Obstacles to recognizing stress in others

Your observation skills have three elements which together influence your ability to recognize when pressure is a problem for others. The first element is knowing what to look for and being sensitive to manifestations of stress. The second is understanding where signs of stress fit into the stress chain reaction. The third is having the ability to observe signs of stress in a clear, objective way. Knowing what to look for without recognizing your own feelings about what you are observing can hinder your perception of events around you. If your attitudes to stress in others are unconstructive and unacknowledged, however hard you look and listen, those attitudes will distort what you see and hear.

How easy do you find it to be observant?

The attitudes which can get in the way of recognizing stress in others are the same as the ones which can get in the way of recognizing signs of stress in yourself. As we saw earlier, the two extremes are the view that stress is a sign of personal weakness and the view that stress is a badge of office.

If you see stress as a sign of weakness you will probably see manifestations of stress in others as a sign of incompetence rather than of inappropriate pressure. You may lose confidence in the ability of the person showing symptoms of stress to do the job adequately, and this can lead to a breakdown in relationships. It can also add to your own pressure level if you believe that because of his or her personal weakness work has to be organized around the stressed person, if a member of staff experiencing stress is seen as being a problem rather than having a problem. The individual may need your help in developing new skills because he or she faces new or different demands rather than because he or she is weak.

Viewing stress as a sign of weakness can lead to an overreaction to any manifestation of stress. Managers who dread having to deal with 'problem people' will have a tendency to minimize any signs that stress is present, and managers who see a full-scale 'mammoth' every time there is a slight hint of pressure problems will exaggerate any sign of stress in a member of staff. In both cases the underlying attitude gets in the way of seeing the stress objectively.

The view that high pressure is a badge of office, almost a status symbol, will similarly make it less easy to use objective observation skills. In this case you will tend to see any signs attributable to a high level of pressure as a normal part of everyday working life. You may even see them as something on which one should be congratulated. For example, if you have noticed that a member of your staff has been working late recently, you may simply commend him or her for the amount of effort being put into the job, and commiserate with him or her about the rigours of life at the top; you may fail to notice the individual's haggard face.

Your past experience of people under too much pressure can also affect your willingness to observe people closely, in case you see the same thing again. This reluctance may be caused by a false assumption that if you do observe signs of stress in someone else you alone are responsible for doing something about it. You may also feel that if you detect stress you will have no choice about whether to take action or not. You do have a choice; making an observation does not mean that you have to take action personally. You have a choice as to how to act on the observation you have made. People under pressure can behave in odd ways and this can be off-putting, as few of us feel totally comfortable dealing with unfamiliar behaviours.

Constructive attitudes help. In this context a constructive attitude recognizes that:
  - Stress is a reaction to inappropriate pressure.
  - Most people experience inappropriate pressure at some time in their working lives.
  - Stress is a fact of life, not a sign of weakness or a status symbol.
  - You can choose how to respond to the observations you make of signs of stress.

Exercise 6.4 will help you review how your attitudes to stress fit with these requirements.

Avoiding jumping to false conclusions: Observation and interpretations

How you deal with the observations you make depends on your personal skills. It does help, though, to recognize that observations are only the starting point to unravelling the stress chain. Your observations of another person's behaviour do not tell you for certain that the person is stressed. At best they will indicate a high probability but you need to check this out. Observation of signs of possible stress does not tell you what is wrong. It is all too easy to confuse observation with interpretation, and interpret the signs we observe as meaning that a person is necessarily stressed. Our interpretation may be unduly coloured by our past experiences. One manager told us of her anxiety when a member of staff developed very bad dandruff. This triggered memories of a previous member of staff with dandruff who had suffered a heart attack attributed to stress. The dandruff was assumed to be an indicator of stress and the manager viewed the present occurrence as proof that the person was stressed. Interpretation is only valid when confirmed by a great deal more information than initial observations can give you.

Another example we know was a manager who observed that a member of staff was frowning more than usual. This was interpreted as a sign of annoyance and the manager came to the conclusion that this person was stressed. In fact, had he checked, he would have learned that the member of staff had just acquired a new pair of glasses and the frowning was part of the process of getting used to them.

Exercise 6.5 focuses on the skills of observation and interpretation, helping you clarify the differences between them.

What to do when you know that there is stress

Once you recognize that the pressure level faced by others is your concern it is easy to fall into the trap of thinking that it is your job to try to remove all pressure from an individual or group. To respond to the work problem of a member of staff by taking it on yourself, in the mistaken belief that by removing the burden you are helping the other person, may be helpful in that it removes a source of stress, but a potential source of challenge, stimulation and learning may well have been removed at the same time. If you indulge in too much of this form of helping the staff will end up stodgy and sleepy and therefore stressed from boredom. A more constructive approach is to consider ways of helping staff to develop their own skills and increase their ability to cope in the future. It is important to consider ways of reducing unnecessary pressure on staff — this is one of the items in the organizational survival guide — but this does not mean removing all pressures by taking on the problems of others.

This strategy of rescuing people from pressure fails for another reason — it increases pressure elsewhere in the organization, usually on you the manager.

The problem has not gone away; it has merely been transferred. In the long run adding to your own pressure in this way would lead to the unproductive situation in which your staff were stressed because they were understretched and you were stressed because you were overstretched.

Your responsibility is to take steps which enable the people who are working for you to spend as much time as possible at their optimum pressure level. This leaves the manager with the dilemma of how to influence the pressure level experienced by staff. You can do this primarily by controlling the settings in which people work and by being concerned with the work they do. Creating the best environment for people to work in involves you in forming and reviewing policies and organizational design, as well as considering how you approach and deal with individual members of staff.

You may want to have a go at the exercises on recognizing stress before moving on to consider the organizational survival guide. To survive, an organization needs to have managers equipped with helping skills to deal with stressed staff. It also needs to take steps to decrease the likelihood of stress in the organization, by reducing unnecessary pressures and becoming fitter to face pressure. You as a manager have an important role to play in creating and using the organizational survival guide.

In the next chapter we will be looking at the helping skills you need when you become aware that individuals on your staff appear stressed.

Exercises for Chapter 6: Recognizing stress in the organization

Exercise 6.1 What to observe in individuals

Observing signs of stress in individuals is a question of knowing individuals' patterns of behaviour and so knowing when they are behaving in an unusual or misplaced way. If you work with all your department closely you may be able to keep an eye on everyone, but if you are responsible for a large part of the organization with a staff too large or too geographically distant to be monitored regularly, you may only be able to monitor those who report directly to you.

Construct a table, using the format shown below, and enter your observations of the normal patterns of behaviour of the members of your staff you know well. Then think about whether you have already noticed any changes in their behaviour when they are under pressure and enter these as well.

Member of staff	Observations of regular patterns of behaviour	How does the behaviour change under high pressure?
Example Hilary	Hilary is a good time-keeper, is methodical and meets deadlines.	Hilary is late, misses deadlines and the work is careless.

Exercise 6.2 *What to observe in groups*

At the group level your observations are likely to be about qualitative rather than quantitative change, but you still need a base-line from which to monitor deviations. Every group has its own characteristics; some groups have regular lively discussion, for example, while others have formal procedures which

Group or team	Observations of regular patterns of behaviour	How does the behaviour change under high pressure?
Example Weekly management team	Lively debate; willingness to confront and challenge; commitment to persevering to solve problems.	Group members unusually polite to each other; no willingness to challenge or confront; nit-picking rather than real problem solving.

damp down discussion. Focus on the group's regular patterns of behaviour, rather than its effectiveness in terms of the purposes for which it was set up. So the first question is: How does this group normally work?

The second question is: How does this group change when under excessive pressure?

You may be a member of, or formally lead, several groups, working parties, teams or task-forces. Construct a table, using the format shown on page 108, and enter the normal behaviour patterns and the changes under high pressure for each group in which you are involved.

Exercise 6.3 *What to observe in organizations and departments*

You will need to decide which indicators are the most useful for your organization or part of the organization, and which kind of comparison to make: over time, or between your organization or department and a comparable one. This may depend on data available to you.

As a start towards formulating your base-line data, write down what you know about each of the following aspects of your organization or part of the organization.

Absence and lateness

What records are kept? What measures would you use for comparisons (e.g., average hours lost per employee per month)? Could you break this down by grade of employee or section? What comparison data could you use? Last year's figures? Another part of the organization?

Sickness

What records are kept? What measure could you use for comparisons (e.g., days lost per employee per month)? Is other data available to you as well as official statistics? Does length of time off sick affect any calculations you would make? Can you compare figures this year with last year? With another part of the organization? Do you have a separate set of data on accidents?

Industrial action

What records do you keep, or have access to, which provide information on strike action, or other forms of industrial action? Do they include 'near misses' where action was threatened but agreement finally reached? Does the data tell you anything useful about what's happening inside the organization, or does it reflect changes outside? What comparisons could you make?

Grievances

What data do you keep or have access to? What procedures do you follow, and does the data record all cases brought or only those that have reached a certain stage? Can the data be broken down by grade or section for comparisons? Can you compare this year with last year?

Staff turnover

What data is kept and what measures are used? Can you separate voluntary severance from firings and redundancy? Does the data show only jobs where replacements have been made or are all leavers recorded? Can you break it down by grade and section for comparisons? Can seasonal adjustments be made if necessary?

Are any of these quantitative measures suitable indices for observing stress symptoms at the organizational level in your organization? Are some more helpful than others? Would personnel data need to be recorded differently if you wanted to pull useful data out? Would changes in records be needed to enable you to spot trends?

How much do the figures fluctuate over the course of a year? What size of fluctuation would you need to observe to recognize that something was happening which deserved greater attention?

What *qualitative* measures would you also look for in your organization?

Reviewing and monitoring should be part of your day-to-day management control activities. However, particularly at the organization level, it is often useful to make a note in your diary or time management system to spend a few minutes making a review on a regular basis. This is particularly important if your review is to include records which will not otherwise be brought to your attention.

Exercise 6.4 *Reviewing your attitudes to stress in others*

It is important to be aware of your views about stress in the organization; when you are aware of your beliefs and attitudes you can recognize when they are affecting your approach to managing pressure. This exercise will help you identify whether your approach to managing stress is positive. The objective is to help you reflect on your *actual* rather than *ideal* position. No one is perfect and we often fall short of doing what we know is best practice. Whether you answer yes or no to the questions below should reflect your approach to date rather than the approach you aspire to.

yes/no

1. Is your immediate response to frequent incidents of industrial action to blame 'the unions'?
2. Do you feel quite happy at the prospect of discussing personal issues and feelings with your staff?
3. If team meetings are going badly do you believe the best policy is to work out whose fault it is and replace him or her in the group?
4. Do you view it as a matter for concern if you detect signs of stress in your staff?
5. Do you believe that high pressure is an integral part of working life and that people must expect work to take its toll?
6. If you notice that a group is not working well, do you take time to ascertain the reasons?
7. Do you avoid talking to people about personal issues or how they feel about their jobs?
8. Do you view it as important to spend time with staff discussing their worth and the pressures they experience?
9. Do you think that signs of stress in your department would reflect badly on you as the manager?
10. If you notice what you take to be signs of stress in a member of staff, do you raise the matter with them?
11. Do you think human resource policies are dealt with by personnel departments and so are not your concern?
12. Do you view a high sickness rate as a matter for concern?

Interpretation

If you answered yes to more odd-numbered than even-numbered questions, it is likely that on balance your attitudes will hinder you to recognize stress in others.

Exercise 6.5 *Observation and interpretation exercise*

The purpose of this exercise is to help you become clearer about the difference between observation and interpretation. This is a distinction which most of us find quite difficult; partly because of the way we use language, and partly because we are used to thinking fast and so do not always recognize when we are interpreting rather than making observations. The distinction is important because false and unchecked interpretations can lead us to take action which is not appropriate to the problem.

To become clearer about the difference, try the following experiment.

The first stage is, at the end of the day, to make some *observations* about the things that have been happening, people you have met, calls you have made, meetings you have had, and so on. What has struck you about today's events? What have you noticed? Either write your observations down or speak into a dictating machine.

Observation	Possible interpretation	Alternative interpretation
Rob looked at his watch every few minutes. Rob kept his coat on. Rob said he had a lot of work to do today.	Rob wanted the meeting over quickly.	Rob thought I would not be interested in what he had to say.
Sally had a clenched fist. Sally had torn up Francis's report. Sally paced up and down.	Sally was furious with Francis.	Work is getting Sally down at the moment.
The client requested another meeting. The client nodded during the presentation. The client asked several questions.	The client's response was favourable.	The client was stalling for time.
The number of phone calls between departments has dropped. Agreement has not been reached on dates for joint project completion. Formal complaints have been made about our department by the other.	The other department has real problems at the moment.	Our manager and the manager of the other department do not get on.

When you have finished, go back through your notes or tape and note whether any of your observations are in fact judgements or interpretations. Observations are things which you can see or hear. Interpretations are conclusions you draw from observations.

The table opposite shows some interpretations along with the observations that prompted them. Analyse any interpretations in your notes or on your tape in the same way.

7. Helping your staff to manage pressure: The skills you need

In this chapter we turn our attention to the first component of the organizational survival guide. As a manager you need to equip yourself with helping skills to enable you to deal constructively with stressed people. We will focus now on the personal skills you need for dealing with staff who are stressed.

Managerial helping skills: Why you need them

Once the individual is showing signs of stress, as a manager you will need to help that person cope with pressure so that he or she can become or remain effective and efficient. This need will inevitably arise from time to time. No one can juggle the balance between pressure and ability to cope so successfully that it is right all the time. Pressures and demands outside your managerial control, as well as fluctuations in fitness to cope, will on occasions defy your planning, however careful, and lead to stressed staff.

The skills you need for helping your staff manage pressure are those which will enable them to deal with their modern-day mammoths. Your skills will help them to form strategies for dealing with the psychological threats they face and the many demands made on them. This is not an easy area for managers to enter, as people frequently try to keep up a poised and unruffled appearance in front of those whose decisions can affect their future. Entry into this arena needs tact and delicacy; and these are not immutable personality traits but involve behavioural skills which can be learned and developed.

Use of these helping skills has a specific aim — effective performance. The manager's objectives are to ensure that staff are working at a pressure level they can cope with, that they are working at their best and that they are challenged, not submerged, by the demands placed on them. The aim is to alleviate the behavioural, mental, emotional and physical changes which are associated with stress and which usually herald a temporary or permanent decrement in performance. People who are away from work with stress-related illnesses are easily identified as temporary non-contributors, but the non-physical effects are just as debilitating. Confused thinking, anxiety and withdrawal, for example, will all affect an individual's standard of work.

You will not obtain good performance from staff or help them cope with stress if your aim is simply to 'keep people happy' or 'keep people ticking over'. Using helping skills does not mean rushing in to reduce pressure by doing things for others, nor being extra pleasant to people when they are stressed. You need skills which help people help themselves. Working at their best will usually make people feel more satisfied with work, and relationships with them may also be easier — these are by-products of successful management of people.

When the ability to cope *exactly* matches the demands made, people feel very comfortable. However, if the demands *slightly* exceed the ability to deal with them but there is still the capacity to cope with the pressure level, then usually the situation is exciting, challenging and energizing. When this is the case people push themselves a little harder to learn and to develop their abilities. This is the point on the pressure continuum for which the manager using helping, or enabling, skills needs to aim. His or her concern is to help people bring their pressure spectrum to that point where they are developing and growing in their work.

To exercise these enabling skills in the face of signs that a member of staff is struggling and possibly stressed, you need to know when helping, or enabling, skills are appropriate. You need to know also what to say and how to talk to people in a way that will have maximum benefit. You need to feel confident in using the skills and comfortable with helping someone who is distressed.

You will need to be assertive: many people find it unsettling to be faced with someone who is not behaving in his or her usual manner. As a result they are too tentative for the other to feel comfortable enough to talk, or too abrasive for the other to respond to the overtures, however well meant. How you feel influences how you approach an individual, and how you feel is influenced in turn by what you tell yourself about handling stress amongst your staff.

When helping skills are useful

Face-to-face helping skills need to be deployed separately from the coaching and appraisal interviews you have with staff, although there are common elements. Other kinds of interview focus on performance issues, and while resolution of problems arising elsewhere may indeed help reduce pressure, a helping interview specifically focuses on a person's experience of stress. It is useful to keep in mind the difference between observation and interpretation, and between cause and effect. At this stage you will not know for certain that someone is suffering from stress; nor will you know what has caused the stress, if any. This is why a face-to-face talk is crucial; you cannot support a person either emotionally or physically if the true position is not discovered. Whilst your inclination may be to rush in and take action, this will be foolhardy until you are sure of the real problems.

Helping skills are also needed in times of major change in the organization or an individual's life, when there is a high probability that the pressure level has risen. As we have seen, change is a considerable source of pressure as people use up adaptive energy to adjust to the new situation. It is likely that at least a few people will be stressed in an organization or department undergoing a restructuring; or where redundancy is happening or threatened; or where there is a major change in direction or style of working; or where working conditions are threatened.

In most organizations the need to communicate information about change is accepted, and managers take great care to pass information to those who need it and to ensure that rumour and ill-informed gossip are kept to a minimum. From personal experience of change, however, most people know that the strong feelings engendered are often conflicting, and resolving them is an important element of adjustment. It is possible to look forward to something new with eagerness one day, only to feel bitter regret at what is being lost the next. Change involves loss — of the old, the established and the familiar — and acceptance of the new, the untried and the unfamiliar.

For someone whose identity is closely allied to a particular organization, set of professional beliefs, or job, retirement, redundancy or uncertainty about the organization's future can be an intense emotional trauma. Life goes on once the crisis has occurred; eventually emotional equilibrium and health are restored when the loss or change is accepted. Figure 7.1 shows the loss cycle associated with major change. Individuals may or may not go through all the phases in the order shown. People can 'miss out' a phase or phases; in this case, before the change is finally accepted they may return to the phases omitted. Failure to do so can leave unfinished the process of acceptance and adjustment. For example, people who are unable to express their anger at a change foisted upon them may find that there is always something which rankles about the new situation.

You can use this model to help you understand what is happening to people when they are adjusting to change. Whilst it is occasionally useful to share this model with someone who is stressed, its main benefit is to help you recognize what is happening so that you do not feel out of your depth when helping people. Unfortunately, knowledge of this process does not stop you experiencing it yourself. Exercise 7.1 helps you draw on your own experience so you can put it to good use when helping others.

The phases are important parts of coming to terms with change. Adapting to change takes time. Since the pace of change is generally accelerating, it is hardly surprising that we all suffer stress as a consequence. People rarely give themselves time to mourn the loss of cherished rituals, traditions or ways of doing things. Using this model, you can distinguish for yourself and your staff the difference between bland reassurance that things will work out all right and real

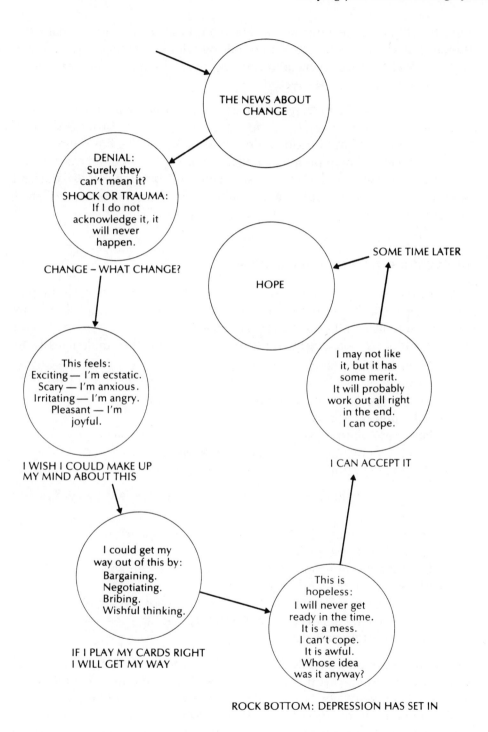

Figure 7.1 Change and loss: The process of adaptation

hope. Real hope for the future comes when one has been able to internalize the change, not when one is merely complying with something imposed from outside. Much change is initiated by others but the individual's process of acceptance needs to be respected.

A brief interview with each person to assess the extent of the problem, and a longer one where necessary, is a good managerial approach to helping people through change. What you do during those talks will be important; bland reassurance will not help people. Change can be welcomed but still stressful. Retirement, for example, is feared by some and welcomed by others, but it is a significant event for everyone and requires adjustment. Whenever there is change you will need your skills to help others cope.

The skills of helping others manage pressure

Helping skills are part of your ordinary repertoire of behaviours. In helping interviews some behaviours are used more often than in your usual discussions with others; similarly other behaviours need to be kept to a minimum. You will be successful at encouraging the other person to sort out their difficulties if you:

- Keep an open mind.
- Listen.
- Accept the other person without being critical.
- Ask open questions.
- Pay attention to feelings.
- Want to understand the other person's view.
- Want to act cooperatively with the other person.

These are features which are positive in the helping interview. You will be less helpful if you:

- Make statements about your own beliefs or opinions.
- Are critical of the person interviewed.
- Concentrate on ensuring that the person is acceptable to others.
- Make evaluations and judgements.
- Attach importance only to the external logic of the situation.
- Take unilateral action without consulting the other person.
- Do most of the talking.

Both of these sets of characteristics are to be found in everyday behaviour; all of them can be useful in your managerial role. You need both to enable you to function in a range of situations — without the second set of behaviours you would probably be regarded as indecisive, overly open to persuasion, and lacking in ideas. It is the setting in which you operate which determines which behaviours are appropriate. If you are helping people cope with problems, the positive features listed above help because they enable people to focus on their own experience, and to explore how they are creating pressure for themselves and what action they want to take to reduce their stress. The other features are less helpful because they result in the manager interpreting the other's experience, rather than helping the member of staff to open up or focus on his or her experience of feeling stressed. Save the behaviours in the second list for times when they are needed — for example, when a quick decision is needed in a crisis and you have the knowledge and the authority to make that decision. Using helping skills often feels like inaction in comparison with other work experience, but the role of helper is active, not passive. It involves a structured approach using a variety of behaviours skilfully, although you may not be 'doing things' in the way you do in other work situations. Once problems have been explored and understood and the individual has decided on a course of action for resolving difficulties, there may well be a further role for you — making things happen, facilitating them and supporting them — but emotional support is necessary first.

The importance of emotional support can be illustrated by the example of a manager in an organization which intends to contract out some of the support services. This had been proposed by one of the directors. The manager we spoke to was faced with a period of uncertainty while the final details of the takeover of the department by the contract company were being finalized. The financial arrangements and career prospects in the new set-up looked good, however, and were virtually certain to be agreed. The manager kept everyone informed of the details as they were communicated to departmental heads. In view of this the manager found it difficult to understand why people kept dropping into the office for a 'chat', and why they seemed highly anxious about the future. Relationships with staff were becoming tense. The manager's view was that everyone knew what was happening; they would have to be patient; there was nothing else to be done; staff and manager had the same information and no one would lose his or her job or long-term benefits. What was the problem? In discussion it became clear that the manager had not understood the stress experienced by people facing major change, even when the change appears to be for the better. Consequently no emotional support had been offered to members of the department: the manager was dealing in logic and facts whereas their experience was emotional. They needed their anxieties to be recognized even if no specific action could follow. They looked to the manager to provide this recognition.

Helping others in four stages

Enabling skills can best be explored using a four-stage model of the overall helping process. Particular behaviours are useful at each stage, although they need not be confined solely to one stage of the process. The basic features outlined previously run throughout the four stages. The four-stage model is illustrated in Fig. 7.2.

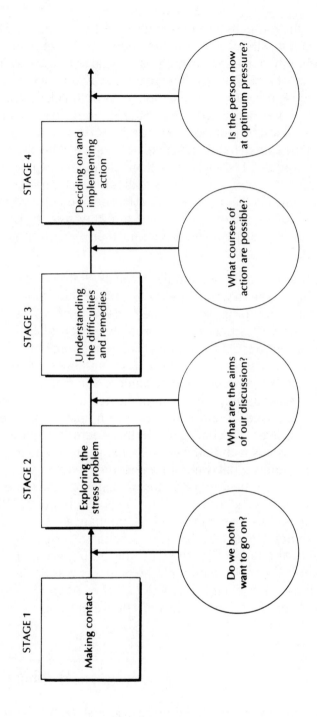

Figure 7.2 The four-stage model for helping others to cope with pressure

After each stage a key question needs to be answered before embarking on the next. Using a model like this provides a framework for your discussion; it gives you a picture of where you are going, so that what you say has direction. Working through the four stages can require anything from a few minutes' talk to months of work spread between a number of meetings. Sometimes you will need to go through the four stages more than once. How long you spend on each stage depends on the problem. Do not rush. The time you spend with staff is an important indicator of the value you place on them and the regard you have for them.

Stage 1: Making contact

You may decide to talk with a particular member of staff, or the member of staff may come to see you. In the example we outlined above, it seemed that people were persistently trying to make contact with their manager; perhaps they were not asserting what they wanted articulately, or perhaps the manager was not very skilled in picking up the fact that they were trying to make contact. You need to recognize an approach and ask what the other person wants from you — what is on his or her mind?

It is perhaps more problematic to initiate a discussion about an individual's stress yourself. If your relationship has been poor, many other changes may be needed before this kind of discussion is suitable. If stress is frowned upon at work, people may not want to discuss difficulties. Pick an occasion on which you will have time to talk if the person responds, but don't keep putting it off until an 'ideal' opportunity arises — it never will.

You need to approach the other person skilfully. If you look unhappy or fidgety he or she may not respond to your invitation to talk openly. If you are initiating a discussion about stress, you have probably so far only your own carefully compiled observations to use as a basis. You may have made some tentative interpretations but you will not have firm evidence for the causes of any changes you have noted; nor will you know the alternative interpretation the other person could attach to your observations. To know about his or her experience you have to ask, and he or she has to be willing to tell.

What you say, therefore, needs to be non-evaluative and non-judgemental, even when your judgements are kindly meant. 'You are suffering stress, how terrible for you', is both an interpretive and an evaluative comment. The other person may initially be unwilling to agree with either element. This could be because your conclusions are wrong; or because the other has not yet acknowledged to him or herself that the stress is present; or because the other is not sure what you are going to do next — offer tea and sympathy or issue a first warning. If you get a rebuff at this stage, you may not be able to recover the situation.

A useful way of handling this first encounter is to combine your observations with some open questions. Open questions are questions which cannot be answered by a simple 'yes' or 'no'; they require elaboration. You could, for example, comment that you have noticed how rushed the other seems, and ask what lies behind it.

You need to say in a non-threatening way that you have observed change and to show that you want to listen. Simply asking if anything is wrong frequently gets a neutral response and so you need to be specific in your opening line. You may need to persist as people often feel reluctant to talk, but do this gently — battering someone's defences down will not achieve your aim of getting a conversation started.

During this stage, which may extend over more than one occasion, your aim is to open up the conversation so that you can establish whether or not it is worth pursuing the issue of stress. You may choose not to start the conversation with the term 'stress'. Indeed it is often wise to avoid the label. Your aim is to make an assessment about the difficulty the person is having and whether he or she will benefit from working through it with you. For it to be of benefit both of you have to be willing to do this.

When to take it no further yourself

You may decide not to continue if the other person is reticent or reluctant. This could be due to their perception of the difficulty, their perception of your interest, how you handle the opening stage or a combination of these. You may decide not to continue if the difficulty the person is experiencing is one which you feel emotionally unable to handle. For example, a death in the family of the other person taking place soon after a death in your own family might be a situation too close to your own for you to talk about comfortably. If this is the case, you may be able to get someone else who is skilled to talk with the other person. Another reason for deciding not to continue might be that you think you do not know enough intellectually about the problem to be much help; for example, you may think you know nothing of bereavement counselling and assume therefore that you have nothing to offer. At this early stage, beware of such assumptions. The person may need you to show recognition of his or her distress, so that he or she does not feel left alone to battle on alone at work. In some instances of serious problems — e.g., alcohol abuse or relationship difficulties — you may encourage the other to seek help from an outside agency. You do not have to solve these difficult problems for your staff; the enabling skills you use will help them to take action for themselves. Usually, too, as the story of the person's difficulty emerges, you will find links in the stress chain reaction which can be broken. You may not be able to do anything about their home difficulty but you may be able to help them sort out enough problems at work for their pressure level to drop.

Where to talk

Another task at this stage is finding a suitable place for discussions — somewhere where you can talk privately without being interrupted. Offices designed so that every sheet of paper turned can be heard by one's neighbour pose a problem. If you have interview rooms or spare conference facilities these are more suitable than the office, as the telephone will not disrupt your talks. Lay the room out so that you can converse without difficulty; avoid confronting your staff member across a desk, for example. Even if there are no easy chairs, seat yourselves at a comfortable distance; using the corner of the desk and sitting around it can help to avoid the feeling of exposure. Sitting at a slight angle to each other enables you to make good intermittent eye contact, without 'eyeball to eyeball' confrontation.

Confidentiality

Finally, you will need to establish early on the degree of confidentiality you are willing to extend to this kind of interview. Your discussion does not have the status of a confessional and there may be issues which arise that you will need to take up elsewhere. You need to make this clear from the start. It is helpful to indicate that any issues raised in the discussion will only be discussed with your manager and only if they relate to specific performance problems. Anything of a personal nature should remain confidential between the two of you, unless you both agree that it should be discussed elsewhere.

Once you have dealt with these initial elements and you both feel happy to move on, it is time to move into the next stage.

Stage 2: Exploring the stress problem

During this stage your aim is to establish a rapport with your member of staff so that the problems can be identified. You need to separate the symptoms from the causes of the problem, and this can take some time to do. You need to gain a full picture of the problem. This may be the first time the person you are helping has sat down with someone to do this. As a result he or she will probably not present him or herself in a very clear and logical way but will need your help to piece together the links in the stress chain reaction.

The first skill is attending and listening. Use body language to convey your interest in what the other has to say. Eye contact, an open facial expression which reflects your feelings as you hear his or her views, an open posture, leaning forward now and then — all these convey your attention. What you say is important too; people need to know that you have really heard what they have been saying. You can let them know you have been actively listening by reflecting back what they have been saying — repeating what they have said if it is brief, or paraphrasing what you have understood them to say. You need to listen carefully for the feelings they express and the needs displayed as well as the content of what they say. Reflecting back is important because it shows that you are attending to what they say and also because you can check that what you heard was correct. Checking for understanding is crucial; people who are under pressure rarely present their difficulties neatly. At this stage you are not concerned with making interpretations.

You will, of course, need to ask questions, but not just any questions. Two kinds are particularly helpful: open questions (Can he or she tell you about what is going on at the moment? Has there been some change that is creating pressure or extra demands for them?); and probing questions. Probing questions can be gentle or the sort of leading questions favoured by interrogators. You need to use the gentle kind! Ask what else happened, what was said on the occasion the other is describing, and so on. Probing questions enable you to fill in the gaps once the picture begins to emerge. They also help the other person clarify the situation. Probing questions are not used to catch the person out. Your approach needs to be concerned; only later if actions agreed on are not implemented need you adopt a firmer stance.

Your task is to move the discussion forward. Having explored the problem the two of you then need to decide what you want to achieve. What should you aim for? Summarizing the discussion so that you can focus on this needs careful timing. The member of staff needs to feel that you have been interested and concerned, not just worried about performance, and often talking itself can help to relieve pressure. You need to decide what aspect, if any, of the overall problem you are going to work on. The goals need to be realistic and limited to things within your joint control.

Keep in mind that the purpose is to reduce the pressure level to optimum, not eliminate pressure. For example, if the picture which emerges is that the stressed person is having difficulty coping with a sick pet at home, an individual on his or her own staff who is not working well, an increase in orders to be processed, and an abrasive newly appointed colleague who is making excessive demands, as well as worries about rumours of redundancy, you will have to decide together what to focus on. Some of the difficulties may seem more suitable for working on than others and if resolved could reduce pressure to a level with which the person can cope. You are unlikely to reduce anxiety and frustration to zero; but that is not the purpose of the helping interview. By the end of this stage you should have established the issues you will work on and what you are hoping to achieve. Both of you need to be clear about this; otherwise you may find that unrealistic expectations are raised.

During this stage it is common for the discussion to cut across the home/work divide. Some people will talk freely about issues which concern them outside work, whereas others see any personal discussion of this kind as an unwarranted intrusion. Your own views on this will also influence the extent to which you raise such concerns, as will how well you know the person. *Your only legitimate area for discussion is the person's behaviour in so far as it affects his or her performance at work* — in one-to-one dealings with others and performance of tasks, in the teams or groups he or she works in, or in interaction with the organization as a whole.

You can insist on exploring only work-related performance and the impact the individual has on the organization. However, because the boundaries between the different parts of the social system are permeable, problems from home are brought to work and pressures at work can be taken home. If the individual brings to work problems from home which then affect how he or she does his or her job, this is of concern to you as a manager. If the individual maintains a rigid distinction between home and work and does not want to discuss matters outside work then it is not your task to pursue them. If outside matters are brought to work, though, it may be appropriate to raise them. It may help to explain why you want to do this, so that people understand that your purpose is to maintain their performance and that you are concerned about them personally, rather than let them assume that you are introducing extraneous problems. Ultimately, the individual decides how much of his or her personal life he or she wishes to share with you (though if external pressures remain and continue to affect the individual's work, you will have to decide what other course of action to take to deal with this).

The issue of confidentiality may need to be clarified at this stage. People need to know whether their discussions with you could affect your future decisions, references or recommendations about them.

Stage 3: Understanding the difficulties and remedies

In this stage you will be focusing on those difficulties the resolution of which will help the individual manage pressure more effectively and reduce (or increase) it to the optimum level. You need to help your member of staff see the themes, broader issues and patterns which emerge from the exploration in Stage 2 and so develop new perspectives on the situations he or she faces. The individual can then move on to decide what to do about them. The skills you need are those which will help the other develop greater understanding of how he or she handles threats and deals with demands. This will also help the individual develop awareness of his or her own responsibility for managing pressure and this can be fruitful when you move on to the action stage.

At this stage the discussion needs to be detailed and specific. You may need to explore people's perception of the situations they face. You may need to be specific about the behaviour they use to deal with difficult situations when under pressure. You may need to help them be clear about the part they play in creating pressure or not being able to cope with it. On the other hand you will also need to take responsibility if you think that you have not met your obligations to the member of staff, or that the organization has failed to meet its obligations. Often the stressed person has only one perspective on the situation and you will need to confront this if you think that there are other ways of viewing it.

Confrontation can appear very threatening unless it is used appropriately — as an invitation to the person you are helping to look at his or her behaviour and its consequences. This may involve encouraging people to see discrepancies and distortions in what they say, or to recognize unpleasant tactics which you have observed them using. You may need to point out strengths which you know they have but which they are not bringing to the current situation. Confrontation in the helping interview can be achieved by making comparisons, for example, between the other person's view and your own. Showing that there are alternative perspectives or that a person's views contain inconsistencies is very different from making an attack on his or her views or beliefs. The purpose is not to prove the other wrong but to broaden his or her understanding.

At this stage you may wish to explore any interpretations you have made, if they still seem to fit the enlarged picture you now have and if you believe that they will help the person see a theme or pattern to what is happening. Themes or patterns which point to a cause underlying an apparently disparate set of problems often help people's learning. If you put forward interpretations for exploration they should be introduced as interpretations, not given the weight of facts or observations.

Finally, you need to progress from understanding the problems to understanding the ways forward. Again you need to see alternatives. At this phase the alternatives for consideration are the courses of action which would resolve the underlying difficulties. These need to be worked on jointly with the other person, and with imagination. Solutions will not always be apparent because the problems to be resolved may have remained untackled for some time, or because the problems do not lend themselves to purely intellectual resolution. The alternatives can range from structural solutions, such as changes in systems or reporting relationships, to personal development goals for the person under stress. Your staff may need both moral and practical support from you.

Stage 4: Deciding on and implementing action

In this stage your role is to help people decide which course or courses of action they will take, based on their better awareness of themselves and the problems. Once action has been decided upon individuals need to feel realistically confident that they can achieve the changes desired. You can help here by guiding them towards identifying the resources and strengths they already have which can be used in the situations currently posing problems. You should work out together a plan of action which is clear and specific enough for the individual to go away knowing what steps to take. It is useful to discuss the costs as well as the gains that he or she can expect so that expectations and reality are well balanced. The plan can include time for review and evaluation with you, and opportunities for a new injection of support from you for actions to be taken.

In this fourth stage, your decision-making and problem-solving skills will be invaluable. Your knowledge of resources may include knowledge of local organizations which can help with specific problems, but usually knowledge of what the work organization itself can offer is your most useful contribution; this can vary from a few hours off work to enable the person to deal with a problem to a major change in role. Some organizations are now using professional counselling services to help managers with issues such as reviewing career direction and progress. If the staff of the service are skilled in other fields of counselling, a referral to an objective outsider of this kind may be useful. Care needs to be taken, though, when making any referral to an outsider. First, the referral must be seen as useful by the person being referred. Second, do not assume that all those in 'caring' professions are either suitable for counselling people who are stressed or would welcome such a task. Some GPs, for example, are willing to do it, but others do not feel skilled or interested in handling people with a stress problem; few have much time available. The same is likely to be true of personnel professionals (who, of course, like you, have an organizational interest anyway). So check before suggesting to members of staff that they take their problems elsewhere.

Sometimes appropriate action involves information or skills which people have not yet learned, so a more directive approach is called for. At this point, for the first time during the helping interview, your teaching skills are required. If it is clear that the person needs either information or to be shown how to do a task then you may wish to help them learn. The teaching skills you need are interactive: show people what to do and then get them to do it with you; check that they have understood what you have explained to them; ensure that they can do it on their own before you finish. Examples of how you might tackle a similar problem can help, but avoid pontification.

Finally, make a point of noticing and commenting when people achieve change. This recognition will be valued in itself but will also help to maintain performance.

Table 7.1 summarizes the separate skills you need for helping people who are stressed to manage pressure. The range is wide but all are good managerial practice. It is important to keep in perspective the purpose of your discussion and to structure the talks. This is useful whether they consist of a brief chat over a cup of tea or longer, in-depth interviews. Exercise 7.2 helps you use the four stages outlined above to prepare and practise helping skills, so that when you approach someone you can be confident that you will say something helpful rather than just want to be helpful.

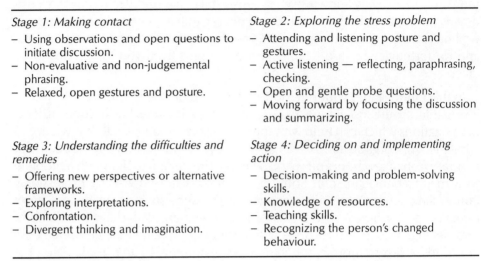

Stage 1: Making contact	Stage 2: Exploring the stress problem
– Using observations and open questions to initiate discussion. – Non-evaluative and non-judgemental phrasing. – Relaxed, open gestures and posture.	– Attending and listening posture and gestures. – Active listening — reflecting, paraphrasing, checking. – Open and gentle probe questions. – Moving forward by focusing the discussion and summarizing.
Stage 3: Understanding the difficulties and remedies	Stage 4: Deciding on and implementing action
– Offering new perspectives or alternative frameworks. – Exploring interpretations. – Confrontation. – Divergent thinking and imagination.	– Decision-making and problem-solving skills. – Knowledge of resources. – Teaching skills. – Recognizing the person's changed behaviour.

Table 7.1 Summary of skills needed at each stage of helping others manage pressure

Using helping skills: Developing confidence

As with any skill, such as assertion, helping skills can be developed. The level of skill you exhibit is influenced by your confidence; a realistic assessment of your strengths and areas of competence is needed. As you practise helping behaviours, which are both verbal and non-verbal, you may find initially that you lose a little confidence and skill. This loss of performance is common, but is a precursor of enhanced skills. The loss is due to your self-consciousness — you are aware of everything you say and do in a heightened way. After a while you will find that you are able to be aware of the behaviours you are using without heightened self-consciousness. After any encounter in which you have practised the skills, you will need to pause and reflect on how you have done. You need to be as objective and as constructively critical of yourself as you would be of people you were helping. Then decide what you would do differently if faced with a similar situation again. Congratulate yourself on the things you handled well and ensure that you remember these when you take stock of your strengths. In a way, you are directing your helping skills towards yourself, with the aim of developing your level of skills.

Obstacles to developing your helping skills

You will have problems using helping skills if you do not deal with your own problems in managing pressure first. If you are struggling to cope you will have little energy available for helping someone else. Without the ability to manage your own pressure and without demonstrating that you think it is important to do so, it is unlikely that your staff will see you as someone they can confidently trust to help them resolve their own difficulties.

Inability to manage your own pressure level may entail your seeing people in distress as one of your modern-day mammoths; or you may find that there are particular situations, such as ones in which emotion is expressed, which seem threatening to you. Like all such 'threats' they need evaluation. You need to know what feature of the situation you find disturbing. One common way of turning an encounter with someone who is distressed into a 'mammoth' is to tell yourself that if someone else is upset it is up to you to put the problems right. This is threatening to your self-esteem because it is generally an impossible task. As we have seen this is not what is needed, anyway, in a helping interview. Alternatively there may be some topics which you find difficult to discuss. Exercise 7.3 will help you think about how far you are prepared to discuss possible mammoths. If any particular type of situation seems fraught with danger to you, check your inner dialogue for faulty thinking and use the information you now have to replace it with some more helpful statements.

It is also difficult to use helping skills if you do not really want to help. You may not want to help for a variety of reasons: you do not like the person very much and feel unsympathetic; you believe people should sort out things for themselves; you would rather treat performance problems as cases for disciplinary procedures; you have tried many times before with no response. Two considerations are important if you do not want to help. First, it is part of your role as a manager to ensure that you do what you can to keep performance at an optimum level; and second, you need to consider whether a helping interview is the best option available to resolve any difficulties. If it is not, whether you want to help or not becomes less of a problem. If it is, you will need to keep the purpose of the interview firmly in mind and keep any negative views you have about it to one side during your discussions.

Hints for good helping skills

There are a number of verbal formulae which can help you achieve your aims in the various stages of the helping interview. Table 7.2 lists a number of these, which you could incorporate in your preparation for a discussion. They are related to the skills you need during the helping interview. Of course, the phrases are only examples of the words you might choose, but it is important that when you speak the choice of words is appropriate for your aim. Table 7.3 gives some examples of phrases that will frustrate your purpose of helping the other person work through his or her difficulties. This is because they are centred on the manager's views and concerns rather than on the person needing skilled help. Exercise 7.4 is designed to help you reflect on any unhelpful habits you may have which will get in the way of using helping skills.

Skill	Formula
Summarizing	– So, the main things we've talked about so far are . . . . – The key points you've made are . . . .
Open questions	– When . . . . ? Where . . . . ? Who . . . . ? What . . . . ? – Can you tell me a bit more about . . . . ?
Active listening	– You seem to feel . . . . because . . . . and what you want (or need) is . . . . – As you see it . . . .
Paraphrasing	– Let me see if I understand you; what you've been saying is . . . .
Probing	– Can you give me an example? And then . . . . ? Did anything else happen . . . . ? – How did that happen?
Confronting	– How are you doing this? – On the one hand you say . . . . on the other hand . . . . – Your view seems to be . . . . whereas mine is . . . .
Alternative frameworks	– Another way of looking at this is . . . . – Viewed differently it could be that . . . .
Checking interpretations	– It seems to me that . . . . Is that how it seems to you? – Could this be what's going on? . . . .
Focusing	– Where we want to end up is . . . . – What seems important is . . . .
Interpreting	– From where I stand it seems that there is a theme here . . . . – It seems implicit in what you're saying that . . . .
Clarifying	– I'm not sure I'm following everything; can you tell me a bit more (or again) about . . . . ?
Divergent thinking	– Let's examine ways in which you could get answers to those questions . . . . – Let's imagine how a variety of people could tackle that . . . . – What other ideas do you have about this? – How else have you tackled these kind of problems? – Where do you think the next step could be? – Where else could you find out about . . . . ? – What would be the consequence of . . . . ? – What hunches do you have that we could follow?
Non-directive information	– I wonder if . . . . could apply to you? – Could it be that this kind of approach would be useful . . . . ? – I think you're not alone in facing this kind of problem . . . . Could x's solution be useful to you? – It is conceivable that . . . . might help.

Table 7.2 Hints for developing skills: Phrases to use when practising the various skills

- What I would do (in your shoes) is . . . .
- Perhaps you could come back when you're less emotional.
- You don't seem very clear about all this; I'd have thought better of you.
- Well, it's time to pull your socks up and get yourself sorted out.
- With respect, your view is quite wrong.
- How on earth can you say that?
- I've done my best to help in the past, but really you don't seem to have improved.
- Are you going to take my advice?
- My advice to you is . . . .
- You seem to be rather weak in this area.
- You'll probably fail on that one.
- You should/would/must/ought . . . .
- Wouldn't you agree with me that . . . .
- Don't you think that . . . .
- Generally speaking, in my experience . . . .
- If I could just interrupt you again to point out that . . . .
- It's obvious to me that the solution is simple . . . .
- Why? Give me your reason for doing . . . .
- A manager in my position can't really . . . .
- People always feel that way . . . .
- You're no different from anyone else around here, you know.

Table 7.3 Hindrances to helping: Examples of phrases to avoid

Your style of helping

One way of thinking about the style you adopt in a helping interview is to reflect on how directive you are with the person you are helping. In a helping interview your style will reflect your own abilities and preferences as well as the stage you have reached in the helping process. Figure 7.3 (on page 132) shows a continuum of styles ranging from directive at one end to reflective at the other.

Typically, as the interview progresses you will need to move from the left of this continuum towards the right. How far towards the directive end of the spectrum you eventually move will depend on factors such as your assessment of the other person's maturity and capacity to develop personally and to learn skills for coping with pressure. If someone's capacity for personal development is currently low he or she may need active and directive help from you, but don't forget that the ultimate aim is to aid people's personal development so that not only can a current crisis be managed but future capacity is enhanced too. Don't rush to the rescue even if you are sympathetic to the issue they face.

Exercise 7.5 helps you assess your style of helping.

REFLECTIVE   DIRECTIVE

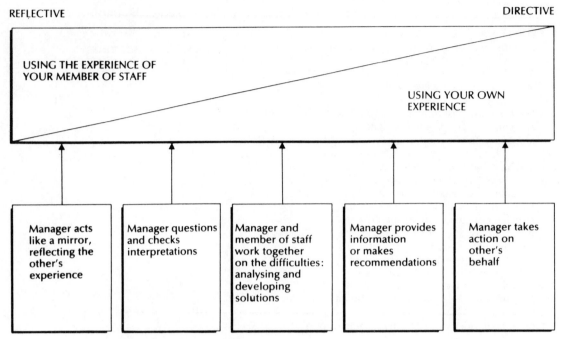

Figure 7.3 Helping styles: The range of options

Developing confidence through practising the skills

In this chapter we have focused on the helping skills you need as a manager, but these are skills which are relevant in other situations too; and you can practise them in other situations as well as managerial ones. They need developing in situations where you can increase both your confidence and your skill level. There is no point in practising helping skills where you have little chance of success. If someone is refusing help then all the skills at your disposal will be of little avail. If you have reached a stage where you feel unwilling to continue because of the nature of the issues emerging, then ploughing on will lead to a loss in confidence. If your past relationship with the person concerned has been fraught, then this may not be the person to practise on.

Once you have made contact and both of you want to talk then prepare yourself thoroughly. Mental preparation means:

- Focusing your attention on the person.
- Planning to use the behaviour you think will be appropriate.
- Making a note of any of your usual comments that you want to avoid in this situation.
- Checking your inner dialogue for faulty thinking.
- Deciding how you will open the conversation if the person says nothing.
- Being clear about the style you want to use.
- Reviewing the stage you have reached and the information you have collected so far.

Finally, take things slowly, so that your thoughts are not continually jumping forward to what you are going to do next or back to what you have just done. If you feel nervous (interviewing of any kind is frequently a modern-day mammoth) do some relaxation for a few minutes. Remind yourself of your purpose. Many people find the intimacy of this kind of interview satisfying, so feel good about this constructive approach to managing stress.

In the next chapter we move on to consider the next element of the organizational survival guide — reducing unnecessary and inappropriate pressure.

Exercises for Chapter 7: Developing your helping skills

Exercise 7.1 Experience of change: The need for support

In this exercise we want to focus on the emotional cycle associated with change, as depicted in Fig. 7.1.

Recall a situation in which a group of which you were part experienced a major working change, such as a reorganization.

What reactions were there?

Can you recall how you felt when you heard about the change? What reactions did you have? What reactions did you observe in the group?

Can you recall how you felt as the change came closer? What reactions did you have? What reactions did you observe in the group?

Can you recall how you felt as the changes were actually introduced? What reactions did you have? What reactions did others in the group have?

How long did it take for you to accept the change? What factors helped you come to terms with it? What about others in the group — did they accept the change? What helped them come to terms with it?

What helped (or would have helped)?

At each stage, what support did you want from your manager or colleagues? What resources did you need?

What information did you want?

What reassurance did you want?

Did you have someone you could discuss your concerns with?

If so, what kind of emotional support did you want from them?

What did other people in the group say they needed? Were these needs different from yours in any way?

What can you learn from this situation?

What can you learn from this and similar experiences which can help you when your staff need emotional support in times of change?

Exercise 7.2 Preparation and practice in helping interviews

It is important when developing your helping skills to enhance your confidence in handling employees suffering stress. To do this you need to prepare carefully for interviews so that you have a structure to follow and can review afterwards how you have done and so plan future improvements in your approach.

A set format such as the one below can help you ensure that your preparation covers all aspects of the interview; after each stage record your notes (for your personal record only) and think about where you want to take the next phase.

Preparation for interview with:

Stage 1

My initial observations: Notes on what _____ said:

My opening statement and question:

When further discussions can take
place:

Stage 2

Open questions I want to ask: Notes on picture of the problem
                                      emerging:

Stage 3

Interpretations I want to check out:

Notes on alternative courses of action considered:

Alternative perspectives I want to offer:

Themes emerging which I want to reflect back:

Stage 4

Courses of action likely to reduce pressure:

Notes on action agreed by — :

Costs and gains of each course of action as I see it:

Actions I have undertaken to do:

Skill development needed for coping:

Exercise 7.3 Mammoths in the office: Are you prepared to discuss them?

In this exercise we review your preparedness to discuss mammoths which could be raised in a helping interview.

Which issues bother you?

Think of your staff and then list the kind of things they grumble about.

Are any of these topics ones you would feel uncomfortable discussing with them? Are any of these topics ones you would not be prepared to discuss with them? Are there any issues or concerns that you generally fear someone raising with you? If so, list them.

   Look over the lists you have just drawn up. Are any of the topics you are not prepared to discuss or are unwilling to discuss also your own modern-day mammoths?

How should you cope with them?

What steps can you take if one of these areas you listed above is raised in a helping interview? Mark those strategies below which are appropriate for you.

	Yes	*Not realistic*
Go back to my own mammoths and spend some time reflecting on how I let an event or person have that effect on me, so that having dealt with it I am able to talk with my staff member more comfortably.		
Refer the person to someone else, knowing who that person could be.		
Set aside my concerns and focus on the other person's, not letting personal views or feelings prejudice my behaviour towards him or her.		
Talk with someone else about my concerns before I engage in any helping interviews.		
Prepare for the interview, incorporating my assertive skills; include in my own inner dialogue a reminder that other people's problems are not the same as mine and that even if the same topic *is* raised I need to recognize that their reactions and interpretations are different and *theirs not mine.*		

Yes   Not realistic

Plan what I will say if one of these topics comes
up; how I will assertively refuse to discuss it without
putting the other down or implying blame.

Other strategies:

Exercise 7.4 Unhelpful habits: Do you have any?

In this exercise we want you to identify any habits or mannerisms that you have,
or phrases that you use, which could hinder your effectiveness in the helping
interview.

Are any of the phrases in Table 7.3 ones which you commonly use?

During the next two weeks be aware as you speak to people of whether there
are phrases, mannerisms or sayings which you *frequently* use. Will any of these
hinder your effectiveness in the helping interview because, for example, they
are centred on you rather than others? Make a note of those habits you will
avoid in helping interviews.

I will avoid saying (e.g., 'Don't bring me problems, only solutions'):

I will avoid doing (e.g., finger-pointing):

Because a manager's job entails making decisions and organizing what
people do and how they carry out tasks, it is easy for managers to fall into a trap
of offering unsolicited, unwanted advice to people experiencing difficulty. It is
often quicker than helping people resolve difficulties in their own time. During
the next couple of weeks be aware of giving advice to others.

How often do you offer unsolicited advice? Every time someone poses a problem or difficulty? Only occasionally? Do you check whether people want your advice? Do you sometimes give them advice when they want a different kind of help in solving a problem? Do you immediately judge ideas others come up with, pointing out difficulties or faulty thinking? Or do you help them see difficulties or faults themselves by asking probing questions and getting them to imagine consequences, or alternative perspectives? Write down your observations of yourself:

Exercise 7.5 Helping interviews: Your style

What style do you think you usually adopt when you help your staff? Decide which point on the scale from reflective to directive corresponds with your customary style; the style you are aware of using most frequently during helping interviews. You may find it useful to refer to Fig. 7.3 when doing this exercise.

REFLECTIVE				DIRECTIVE
1	2	3	4	5
I act like a mirror reflecting experience	I question and check interpretations	We work together on the difficulties: analysing and developing solutions	I provide information or make recommendations	I take action on the other's behalf

Now decide the point on the scale which represents the style you would prefer to use most frequently in a helping interview. This may or may not be the same as your customary style. If there is a difference between your customary style and the style you would prefer to use, you will need to bring the two into line.

What behaviours do you want to use more of?

Which behaviours do you want to avoid?

8. Reducing unnecessary and inappropriate pressure: Mammoths in the office

To provide the next element of the organizational survival guide, we consider ways in which you can reduce unnecessary or inappropriate pressure within your organization. Although a certain level of pressure is needed for optimum performance by all levels of an organization, unnecessary or inappropriate pressure increases the likelihood that part of the organization will experience stress.

Reducing unnecessary pressure means stopping practises which put pressure on people and which are unhelpful to performance of the key tasks and roles which these people fulfil. Organizational practises which are inappropriate for the jobs to be done, which neglect human needs and which frustrate people's sense of achievement all put unnecessary pressure on members of the organization. Rather than raising people to a suitable level of arousal for best performance, this kind of pressure drains their energy for coping with pressure. The resultant mismatch between demands and capacity will result in stress and will call for the use of the helping skills we outlined in the last chapter. There will always be pressure; your job is to ensure that it is of the kind that works for the organization, not against it.

You can influence the pressure level by assessing whether your own behaviour and style creates unnecessary pressure for your staff; by identifying and taking steps to alter the inappropriate core values and beliefs which influence the organization; and finally by recognizing when organizational life frustrates the needs of staff. These are the three issues we will be exploring in this chapter.

Table 8.1 shows some commonly quoted causes of stress in organizations. This list will not necessarily look very different from the one which you drew up for yourself when we were considering stress and the individual manager. You may on the other hand find it hard to understand why some of the items are seen as difficult. When you investigate the sources of stress for others you are searching for other people's modern-day mammoths. A situation which appears highly threatening and dangerous to someone else may seem routine and unimportant to you. Problems which kept you awake at night in the early part of your career may now seem like simple everyday matters; for some members of your staff they may still pose difficulties.

- Too much work.
- Uncertain career prospects.
- Terrible meetings.
- Difficult colleagues.
- Atmosphere at work.
- Poor pay.
- Too much happening.
- Open-plan offices.
- Covering for people off sick.
- Not knowing how I am doing.
- Nobody asks me anything and nobody tells me anything.

Table 8.1 Common sources of stress in organizations

There is, however, one possible addition to the sources of stress for your staff, which will not have appeared on your list of sources of stress for yourself. Among the modern-day mammoths stalking the office may, just possibly, be you. You may not think of yourself in this way, but if you are managing people it is highly likely that for some of them, some of the time, you will appear large, shaggy and tusked. To some extent this is beyond your control, but there are things you can do which affect, for better or worse, your threatening qualities.

How you can cause stress in others: The manager as mammoth

We considered how you can create pressure for yourself in Part 1. In this section we want to focus on how you can put unnecessary or inappropriate pressures on others by the expectations you hold about how they should act at work, by inappropriate beliefs about the exercise of authority, and by the way you act at work yourself.

What do you expect from others?

As a manager you will expect your staff to do their job to the best of their ability. That is not what we mean when we talk about your expectations of others possibly exerting inappropriate pressure. You may be expecting them to do too much and carry a workload which exceeds their abilities, and this may be an avenue to explore if your staff are experiencing stress, but it is often the expectations you hold about the *way* people should do their jobs and behave at work which are the source of unnecessary pressure. You will of course expect your staff to spend their time working while at work, but the definition of what constitutes work activity can vary considerably. One local government manager, for example, worked himself into a fury whenever he saw a member of staff reading a newspaper at work. He could not accept that local newspapers were a valuable source of information for his department. He had a rigid belief that reading newspapers could not be work. Another example we came across was a manager who passed two members of her staff on the stairs catching up on the latest developments of a particular project. Her view was that this was gossip and not work, because she believed that if the information was important it would be brought to a formal meeting. These expectations about the formal nature of work put a lot of pressure on her staff because it cut them off from important sources of information and social support.

Expectations about what constitutes work will often be accompanied by expectations about how work should be done. You may expect your staff not only to work to the best of their ability but to get every detail right. If you have an expectation of perfect work at all times, it will be harder to deal objectively with any mistakes made by your staff. It will put pressure on them to check every little detail, making sure that every 't' is crossed and every 'i' dotted, even when such attention to detail is not necessary. Staff will also try to cover up any mistakes they make, and will tend not to discuss ideas in an early stage with you because they know that you like ideas to be perfectly worked out before you consider them. Such an expectation of perfection is unrealistic, and thus inappropriate.

Another possible source of pressure for your staff may be an expectation that as people know how to do their job they should get on with it on their own, without support. One comment we have heard which illustrates this attitude is that a competent professional does not need to work in a team; and another is that people who have been trained professionally should not need further development. Obviously you do not expect people to come to you for help with every task they undertake but everybody needs assistance and support at some time or other. Expecting people to 'stand on their own two feet' at all costs and at all times is a way of putting pressure on them.

A common expectation is that staff must always consider the needs of others or the organization, not themselves. Balancing the needs of individual members of staff with the needs of the organization as a whole is not always easy, but expecting staff to ignore their own needs puts pressure on them. It does not solve any problems; it merely leads to staff getting the message that they do not matter to the organization. Eventually they may make their needs or wishes clear in no uncertain way — and often a disruptive way. For example, cutting back on off-the-job training for staff because your department is facing a heavy workload at the moment broadcasts the message that staff are less important than organization needs. This may make staff doubt that their career ambitions can be achieved in the organization, and in the long term it may be damaging to the department, as morale drops.

You may have the expectation that your staff put as much effort into their job as possible. However, to emphasize the effort rather than the achievement of tasks puts pressure on people to expend amounts of effort which may not be necessary. Alternatively they may feel obliged to pretend they have put in a lot of effort, and may even be worried by the ease with which they did a task. The message they have received is that they are not skilled enough and that you believe they should put in a lot of effort to compensate.

The other side of the coin is the expectation that the speed at which people work is important, rather than the amount of effort. Both effort and speed matter. It is the unrealistic emphasis on one to the exclusion of the other which causes difficulties. If you expect your staff to rush through their work at top speed, you are also likely to give them a workload which is too heavy to handle comfortably. If you do this consistently, not just in the occasional crisis, you will be a source of considerable pressure to your staff.

Passing tensions on to others: The 'busy' manager

You do not have to insist others behave in accordance with your beliefs to put unnecessary pressure on them; you can do this by your own behaviour. You can pass pressure on to others, perhaps inadvertently, when you yourself are stressed. It is as though the stress you create for yourself can 'infect' other people through your behaviour and the tense atmosphere you create.

There is a very common behaviour pattern amongst managers which can lead to a high-pressure atmosphere. This is the 'busy' manager. Table 8.2 outlines some of the most common behaviours of such a person. There are three main elements: an emphasis on speed; a high level of activity; and a competitive and somewhat ruthless approach. The 'busy' manager is always on the go, always rushing, often scurrying along a corridor, and tends to be a workaholic. 'Busy' managers are extremely competitive, even when cooperation is required, and frequently use aggressive behaviour. They strive for achievement, but rather than being pleased when they have reached a goal, they immediately seek another. A sense of struggle gives them excitement and direction. Such people need to feel that they are always moving onwards and upwards. They constantly seek greater challenges and risks to pit themselves against. To enhance the sense of struggle and striving they will set themselves very tight deadlines, take work home and take on more and more work.

- Speed — speaks quickly, thinks quickly, moves quickly.
- High level of activity — takes on more and more work.
- Takes work home.
- Strives for achievement.
- Seeks new challenges.
- Sets tight deadlines — works better when deadline is imminent.
- Impatient.
- Underestimates time needed for a task.
- Competitive.
- Aggressive.

Table 8.2 Common behaviours indicative of a 'busy' manager

Time is of the utmost importance to 'busy' managers. They are very impatient when work is not done on time, for whatever reason. They find it hard to accept that not everyone will share the 'busy' pattern. They want to get the most out of every moment; they speak quickly, think quickly and act quickly. You can often detect 'busy' managers by the speed at which they act, rather than what they do or achieve. Unfortunately the 'busy' manager will tend to underestimate the amount of time a particular task takes. Consequently he or she will take on too much.

'Busy' managers seem to be hooked on adrenalin; they appear to need the buzz it gives. One way of ensuring sufficient adrenalin is to leave jobs until the deadline is imminent. This eleventh-hour approach is one way in which 'busy' managers put pressure on themselves.

Not only does the 'busy' manager put himself or herself under a high degree of pressure, thus increasing the likelihood of an early heart attack; he or she will also put pressure on others. Because 'busy' managers are always on the go, there is a common view that they must also be performing well. This is not always the case. It becomes less so as people rise through the organization because 'busy' managers do not leave time to stop, think and plan. Many organizations appoint senior managers on the basis of the myth that 'busyness' means achievement, but 'busy' managers at the top only succeed in creating a high-pressure organization, not necessarily a productive one. Exercise 8.1 at the end of the chapter is designed to help you identify whether you are a 'busy' manager.

Causing pressure by how you exercise authority

From the early messages you received and past work experience you will have acquired views about how to exercise authority, and expectations of how others should respond. These assumptions will be very powerful, whether or not they are appropriate to the present situation.

We all learn very early in our lives what it is like to be on the receiving end of authority, as well as how people act when they are in authority. When you are in a hierarchical organization it is easy for these past experiences to influence your present behaviour. This can happen even when it appears on the surface that you are an equal partner, as in a management team meeting. The issue of authority and hierarchy is still relevant.

Some people believe that, to be able to lead, direct, and administer discipline, a manager should remain distant from staff and not get too friendly. Others believe that people in authority should get to know those they manage. Managers believing the latter will behave quite differently towards their staff from managers taking the former view. Both views are appropriate in certain settings; problems arise when they govern behaviour regardless of the setting.

You will also have views about how subordinates should act. Respect and loyalty are examples of commonly held expectations of staff. If you expect your staff to treat you in a certain way regardless of the situation, or of their needs or the needs of the job, this will put pressure on them. Your staff will have their own views about how they should be managed.

We will now consider how the beliefs and values held elsewhere in the organization can cause unnecessary pressure.

How beliefs and values exert pressure in organizations

Every member of an organization has core beliefs and values which affect behaviour at work. Groups in the organization as well as the organization itself will also have clear views about how people should behave at work. Understanding how these various views can bring about unnecessary pressure will help you deal with it.

How you can influence expectations held by staff which cause pressure for them

Your staff will vary in what they perceive as mammoths. They will also differ in their proneness to seeing threats and difficulties. Some people will have thoughts and feelings which predispose them to seeing modern-day mammoths. People with low self-esteem, high anxiety and little belief in their own ability to influence events will be likely to see a lot of problems. On the other hand people with high self-esteem, low anxiety and a belief in their own ability to influence events will be less likely to see events as threatening. The beliefs your staff have will affect the way in which they see themselves at work and, if inappropriate, will add to the pressures they face.

The beliefs people bring to work may be surprising to you, and even clash with your values. If people believe, for example, that they should do things quickly whereas you expect them to take their time and put in a lot of effort, conflict seems inevitable.

It is useful to consider how much, or how little, influence you can have over the values and beliefs held by others. However unrealistic the expectations people bring to work, you cannot actually change their views for them. They have to do this themselves, though you may be able to help by giving them some assistance in assessing whether a particular expectation is appropriate and in deciding whether and how to change it. By using the skills we discussed in the last chapter you can help your staff re-evaluate the pressures they place unnecessarily on themselves through the beliefs and values they hold.

How you can influence expectations held by a group which cause pressure for it

A working group can form beliefs which are more than the sum of the views of the group members. From the moment of its inception a team will develop values and expectations about how its members should operate in the group. For example, there will be expectations about how contributions are made in meetings, the process by which discussions should proceed, how the chair should be addressed. There will also be expectations about the standard of dress expected of group members, the style in which papers are to be written and the style of communication. Such expectations can be central to the way the group works, in which case all members will be expected to conform to them: or they may only be peripheral, in which case it will be considered desirable for members to conform to them. The most powerful expectations will not be formal or recorded in any procedures or rules; they will be informal but nevertheless known to all group members. A newcomer to the group has to learn these values without ever having them explicitly spelled out. There will be a great deal of pressure on people within the group to conform to these group norms.

Where the group norms clash with individuals' values or expectations, or hinder the achievement of tasks, they will act as a considerable source of pressure. The pressure to conform can override the group's normal decision-making processes and lead to strange behaviour at times. The group may stop listening to people whose views are at variance with the one the group is proposing; it may narrow discussion to only a few courses of action so that dissent is minimized; or it may stop taking account of people outside the group, thereby creating a false sense of cosy harmony within the group. The group norm operating in this case is that a group must always be harmonious and that the way to achieve this is to avoid dissent. This is unrealistic and a source of pressure to group members because true harmony and consensus do not come from ignoring or discarding unwelcome views, but rather through full discussion and challenging confrontation. Many groups operate on the assumption that disagreement between members must be avoided at all costs, an assumption often based on the notion that disagreement will lead to unpleasantness as well as being unproductive. This is an inappropriate expectation which will be a considerable source of pressure.

One of your roles as a member of a team is to help the team to be open about the norms guiding group behaviour, and to help them assess these norms and, if necessary, alter them. The first part of Ex. 8.2 is designed to help you do this.

How you can influence organizational values which cause pressure

At a wider level an organization also forms views and beliefs about the way it should operate. In some organizations the prevailing values can be traced back easily to the founding individual or family, though the stories about the founders' beliefs may be based on myth rather than fact. Some of these values may be embodied in the formal structure and policies of the organization today, but often they will be present at an informal level, embodied in legends which have grown up about the founders and their values or actions. Such beliefs and values are pervasive and very powerful determinants of how things are done in the organization. Other strong individuals in the history of an organization can also influence its culture. It is not unusual for people to hark back to the past, when a particular person was in charge and the organizational culture was being formed. You may be in an organization where the process of establishing organizational values is still going on. These are likely to be more appropriate to the current situation facing the organization than those inherited from many years ago and never re-evaluated.

Often organizational values are implied rather than explicitly stated, though currently many organizations are making explicit the values, beliefs and expectations they want to permeate the whole organization. Whether implicit or explicit, organizational values will exert pressure on every member of the organization.

Your role in reducing unnecessary pressure can be to help the organization identify the implicit values and beliefs which guide its policies, strategies and design, and to help it assess whether they are appropriate for the present situation. The second part of Ex. 8.2 will help you do this.

Outdated views and unrealistic expectations will create unnecessary pressure within an organization at all three levels: that of the individual, that of the group, and that of the organization as a whole. Implicit in the design and strategy of an organization are views about the importance of staff and work teams. If there is a view that the needs of people are unimportant within the organization, those needs will often be frustrated and unnecessary pressure will accumulate. Frustration often finds expression as symptoms of stress. Let us now consider ways in which an organization can frustrate the needs of its members.

Frustration: When people do not get what they want or need

One of the main ways in which an organization can cause unnecessary pressure is by frustrating the needs of its staff. Not everyone wants or expects the same from work. For some people it is the financial rewards which rate highest on their list of priorities. For other people it is the chance to be part of a team which matters; whereas for others it may be the cut and thrust of a busy and successful organization which is important. You may have a clear idea of what your staff want from their jobs, or you may not be so sure. A survey would probably reveal a wide variety of different aspirations, but if the organization, through its policies, structure or climate, acts to frustrate the needs of the individual, this will lead to stress.

Most managers are only too well aware of the problems which can arise when they have staff who do not fit the job they hold. The expression 'a square peg in a round hole' expresses vividly the mismatch which can occur when the demands of the job do not match the individual post-holder, for whatever reason. Organizations go to great lengths during the selection process to fit people to jobs, through detailed job descriptions and post-holder specifications, yet problems can still arise. The wrong person in post is an obvious way in which pressure can build up within an organization. People may be unsuited for jobs by reason of skill, inclination or personal characteristics or because the jobs do not provide the satisfaction they seek from work. Job satisfaction occurs when the organization requires from the individual the skills and talents he or she possesses and wants to use, and in return provides recompense. Recompense for expenditure of energy takes various forms, of which the most obvious is money. Yet few people work for money alone. People enjoy work because the job provides satisfaction of the three basic needs: for contact and recognition; for variety and stimulation; and for structure and stability.

Whenever the basic needs are not met, whenever there is a lack of recognition, variety or stability, staff will experience the pressure of frustration. 'Frustration' is a word which is often used to describe the experience of stress as well as the causes. However it is used, whenever there is frustration within an organization there will be an increase in pressure, and therefore potential stress.

Paradoxically, frustration can occur when there is an abundance of contact with others, too much stimulation and too rigid a structure, as well as when there is a lack of these things. For optimum performance there needs to be an optimum level; too much or too little can both cause problems.

People differ widely in the level and type of recognition they want, the level of stimulation which suits them, and the structure they require for optimum performance, but if any of these needs are not satisfied in the organization frustration will follow.

We are not suggesting that as a manager you ascertain the specific desires of each member of staff and redesign work to suit each individual, but if you take account of the many ways in which the working environment frustrates the three basic needs and take steps to avoid unnecessary pressure due to frustration, it will reduce the potential for stress within the system.

How to avoid frustrating the need for recognition and contact

The need for recognition and contact can be frustrated in an organization in many ways. Even though people differ in the amount of contact they require, a job which offers little or no contact with others is potentially stressful because of the isolation which is experienced. People can be physically isolated because of the layout of offices or because they are surrounded by noisy machinery. It is possible to be psychologically isolated by being left out, not told about important issues or taken account of. At the other extreme staff may be involved in work which constantly brings them into contact with others, with little time on their own. The phrase 'people poisoning' has been coined to describe the experience of feeling inundated with the demands of social interaction. This will be heightened when the contact is frequent and temporary. Each interaction is demanding and an excess can lead to overload. It is hardly surprising that people in this sort of job occasionally exhibit less than good humour. Examples of jobs where people poisoning is common are reception work and dealing with enquiries or complaints. An excess of interpersonal but impersonal contact is potentially stressful.

The reason why a certain quantity and quality of contact with others are needed is that it is primarily face-to-face dealings with other people that satisfy the need for recognition. Recognition can take various forms. At its most intense it is good to know that someone likes or loves you. At less extreme levels everyone needs to know that their efforts are acknowledged by others and that their work is appreciated. At the very least we all need recognition of our presence. One of the most distressing experiences for anyone is to be ignored by others. If you are ignored you are discounted. To be treated as if you do not exist implies that you do not matter. We all need to know that we matter and are valued by others.

An organization can frustrate the need for recognition by acting in ways which deny the individuality and worth of its staff or their work. Table 8.3 shows some ways in which this can happen, often inadvertently. It is as if the organization unconsciously adopts a policy that staff do not matter. If this message is received, recognition will be sought elsewhere or in ways which guarantee attention. If positive recognition is not forthcoming from an organization this can often lead to people acting in ways which provoke negative recognition. Negative recognition is better than being ignored or

---

- No individual achievement recognized.
- Lack of recognition for team's achievement.
- Isolated working.
- Excess of impersonal contact with people.
- Stereotyping.
- Formal, impersonal climate.
- Putting staff in low-status positions.
- Little interest in career and development of staff.
- No merit schemes.
- Detailed disciplinary and grievance procedures, with no 'congratulatory' procedures.
- Rewards not based on merit.

Table 8.3 Ways in which an organization can frustrate the need for recognition and contact

treated as if you are unimportant. At the extreme, when you are being disciplined formally you know that the organization recognizes your existence, whereas it may previously have given little indication of being aware of your presence.

An organization frustrates the need for recognition when it does not recognize achievement; for example, when its promotion policies are based on years of service, rather than merit, or when the salary structure does not offer any scope for financial recompense for achievement, such as merit increments. The old adage that it is not what but whom you know operates in some organizations, and this will be seen as unfair by many people as it fails to provide recognition for performance.

The lack of a system of positive recognition for achievement is often felt more sharply when it contrasts with a detailed system for dealing with disciplinary matters. This is not an argument for paying less attention to disciplinary matters, but rather a suggestion that equal attention be paid to recognizing achievements. As one manager put it, 'My organization has a disciplinary procedure; it does not have a congratulatory procedure.' Disciplinary procedures are needed to deal fairly with performance problems when they threaten the effectiveness of the organization, but similarly congratulatory procedures are needed to prevent frustration.

Money is not the only mechanism by which an organization provides recognition. Company cars, titles, office accommodation, expense allowances, medical facilities and various 'perks' of the job are all ways of recognizing the value of staff. The status accorded to a person within the hierarchy is a direct recognition of the organization's view of their worth. Frustration can occur when a person's status is low.

The climate and prevailing ways of behaving within an organization are an important, though less tangible, factor in the recognition of individuals. If the climate is formal with emphasis on impersonal and distant relations between staff, or if social contact between staff is discouraged, there will be less opportunity for recognition. Equally, if there is a view that individual concerns, either regarding events outside work or future career development, are not relevant to the organization, and attention is restricted to the present performance of a job, the individual as a whole person will not be recognized. Although the immediate concern is necessarily performance in the job, as we have demonstrated, pressure from a variety of sources can influence present performance. If people are concerned about some aspect of their life outside work, their work may well be affected.

We have met many managers who have explained a lack of concern with a person's life outside work as based on a desire not to pry. Obviously the right to privacy should not be violated, nor are we advocating the Japanese approach whereby the organization controls most of the life of their staff; we are suggesting that one way to give recognition to members of staff is to recognize that they do have concerns beyond the immediate performance of the job.

Another reason often given for an organization's lack of recognition of staff is the belief that too much praise will lead to an overinflated ego. Unfortunately this can lead to an emphasis on self-effacing and unassertive behaviour, in the belief that modesty is a virtue. Realistic assessment of strengths and weaknesses should be encouraged. False modesty, either in the form of public denial of strengths or private exaggeration of weaknesses, does not encourage good performance. An organization which publicly emphasizes mistakes or encourages false modesty does not satisfy the need for positive recognition.

Lack of recognition for an individual within an organization can also come from stereotyping, in which the way a person is treated is based on a set of beliefs unfounded on reality. Organizations can fail to recognize people's worth or individuality when it stereotypes them on the basis of race, gender or profession. Professional groups are often stereotyped, as are particular functions within an organization. There is often a view that, for example, all personnel staff are, or should be, kind and caring individuals, and members of the personnel department are treated accordingly. While perhaps flattering, it will nonetheless disregard the reality, which is that personnel staff vary in this respect, like any group of people. Stereotypes about the accountancy or finance department may include the equally unfounded belief that all accountants are hard, uncaring people whose only concern is money. Stereotyping within an organization denies recognition in that it superimposes a view which is not based on evidence or information from a person. It denies the individual by emphasizing characteristics expected of the role. The role a person fills at work is important, but when treatment of that person is based on a stereotyped view, the individuality of the person occupying the role is not recognized.

Individuals also get recognition, positive or negative, through their membership of the organization. In the current climate, many managers in public-sector organizations, for example, feel that they are receiving excessive negative recognition which acts as a source of pressure. It is better to be on the receiving end of criticism than to be ignored, but everyone still has a need for positive recognition. Being part of a successful organization or profession that is recognized for its achievements is a very powerful source of satisfaction. Being part of a profession or organization which is not successful or highly regarded is frustrating. Organizations and professional bodies need to highlight their successes.

Work groups can also satisfy or frustrate the need for recognition. Membership of a group or section which has high status and respect within an organization is rewarding, whereas the knowledge or perception that the groups you work in are not highly regarded is frustrating. Recognition can be withheld from a group by not taking account of its work, giving it low-priority tasks or isolating it geographically.

A work group can also frustrate its members by not recognizing individual concerns within the group. If there is little or no interest expressed in the individual members and their achievements on behalf of the group, frustration will occur. Lack of concern with individuals and unsatisfactory relations between group members often indicate a stressed group. When a group is stressed it can add to the pressure already experienced by frustrating the members' need for recognition.

Your staff will not only look to the organization or the team for recognition; they will also look to you as their manager. Whether you satisfy this need will depend on two factors. First, the way in which you give recognition to your staff through your behaviour is important. Thanking a person and commenting on a piece of good work is an obvious way in which you can give personal recognition. Less obvious is the recognition you give through your use of time. If you are always busy and have little time to spend with your staff it will often be interpreted as a lack of interest or concern, and therefore a lack of recognition.

The second factor which will influence the amount of recognition you give to your staff is the beliefs you hold. We have met many managers who have expressed the view that commenting on a person's work is pointless, as people are only doing their job. This may be so, but if they are doing it well and this is not recognized, they will feel frustrated. Another common concern is that if managers tell staff whenever they are pleased with a piece of work, praise or recognition will become meaningless. The belief is that if you give someone too much positive recognition, it will in some way devalue the currency. There is a grain of truth in this view. If you comment effusively and inappropriately on every action a person performs, your praise becomes meaningless and no longer satisfies the need for recognition. A person can get too much recognition if the recognition is of the wrong kind. An excess of negative attention, criticism or blame only frustrates, as does an excess of effusive or insincere congratulations.

Exercise 8.3 will help you identify whether the need for genuine positive recognition is being met in your organization and, if not, what you can do about it.

How to avoid frustrating the need for variety and stimulation

Everyone has a need for a certain amount of variety, challenge and excitement within their lives. Table 8.4 shows some of the ways in which an organization can frustrate this need. Frustration will occur when work provides little variety and stimulation. Too much stimulation and too many demands can also be frustrating. In all organizations there are routine and boring tasks which must be completed if the organization is to achieve its objectives, but it is not necessary for all these tasks to be concentrated in one job.

- Routine jobs.
- No challenge in work.
- Too much to do.
- Tedious meetings.
- Repetitive workload.

Table 8.4 Ways in which an organization can frustrate the need for variety and stimulation

An extreme example of how work can cause the stress of boredom is assembly-line work. If a person does the same task repeatedly for many hours at a stretch with little to break the monotony, it is not surprising that anything which provides some stimulation or variety is welcomed. A job may provide plenty of activity but little challenge. Having little to do frustrates the need for stimulation, but being busy is not a guarantee of variety.

People differ in the amount of stimulation they need for optimum performance. An excess of stimulation, too much variety and too much activity to handle comfortably will also be frustrating. A job which demands rapid switching of attention from one task to another overloads the system and becomes stressful.

Unfortunately many organizations inadvertently frustrate the need for variety and stimulation by a strict adherence to the principles of efficiency. Scientific methods for measuring work and identifying efficient work output are valuable, but the drawback of this approach is that it often regards human resources in the same way as material resources and plant. Efficiency in people depends on more than bodily factors. It may be possible physically to perform a task so many times an hour, but it may not be psychologically satisfying. Using resources in the best way to achieve organizational objectives depends on satisfaction of the need for stimulation and variety.

Organizational life can also be frustrating, not only in the content and design of jobs but also through the cultural expectations of behaviour. A view that no one should step out of line or 'rock the boat' will encourage conformity. If this is taken to extremes it can stifle innovation, creativity and challenge. Individuals seek variety in many ways, some of which can be unconstructive in the organizational setting. If the organization does not provide enough stimulation and expects members to be content with routine tasks, people will often attempt to provide variety for themselves by negative behaviour, such as causing a row, or sabotage. One way in which stimulation can be generated is by openness to new ideas. If these are suppressed, boredom can result.

A group can also frustrate the need for variety and stimulation if its meetings are tedious, or follow predictable, even ritualized, procedures.

Exercise 8.4 will help you identify whether the need for stimulation and variety is being frustrated in your organization, and, if it is, what you can do about it.

How to avoid frustrating the need for structure and stability

The third basic need we all have is for a certain amount of stability and predictability in our lives. Everyone needs variety; at the same time there is a need for some areas of stability. Structure — in terms of time, environment, relationships or work — is essential to well-being. An organization can fail to satisfy this need either when there is too little stability or when it becomes over-structured and rigid. Table 8.5 shows some of the ways in which an organization can frustrate this need.

- Little individual autonomy.
- Inflexible procedures.
- Ambiguous roles.
- Conflicting demands.
- Frequent organizational restructuring.
- Little organizational direction.
- Little account taken of effect of organizational changes.

Table 8.5 Ways in which an organization can frustrate the need for structure and stability

When there is little direction given from senior management, people within an organization will feel there is little purpose to their work. Strategic values and guidelines are the first way in which an organization structures work experience. It also structures relationships into the form shown on the organization chart, which indicates the network of relationships and contacts, as well as accountability and reporting relationships. Where relationships are unclear or ambiguous, frustration can all too easily set in. An organization also provides a physical structure in its offices and buildings. A physical environment which is unsatisfactory because of overcrowding or an uncomfortable temperature, poor ventilation or noise can also be stressful. The physical environment of a job is more important than is recognized in many organizations. The prospect of an office move or a change to open plan offices is often seen as threatening, because the familiar physical structure of work is being disturbed.

Organizational change is the main way in which an organization can frustrate the need for stability. A change in tasks, additional responsibility or a reorganization can often lead to intense discomfort. Unfortunately many organizations view restructuring, either of the whole organization or parts of it, as a main way of solving problems. We are not suggesting that organizational change should never occur, for that would lead to rigidity, but all too often restructuring is an inappropriate or unnecessary step. We met one manager who commented, 'It is most unusual, we have not been reorganized for nine months now.' This showed a rather cynical acceptance of the organization's policy of achieving its objectives by continually searching for the perfect organizational structure. Reorganizations are often necessary, but frustration can be caused when the effects on staff of the upheaval are not taken into account.

At the other extreme an organization can frustrate the need for a certain amount of structure and stability by working within a rigid and rule-bound system. In this case there will be little individual autonomy. Choices about what tasks to do, when to do them and how to do them will be restricted if there is no flexibility in the organization. A culture which dictates that everything must be done by the book can inhibit individual freedom and be too structured for satisfaction.

A work group can also frustrate its members' need for structure by being rigid in its working or, on the other hand, having too many elements of ambiguity for comfort. A group with no clear task to perform, with unclear boundaries and changing membership, with no clear authority, will soon start to function badly, if at all. There will not be enough structure. On the other hand a group which overdefines the roles of its members and allows no deviations from its rules will be restrictive rather than stable.

You as a manager can influence the structure and stability in the workplace, in particular through the way you structure the time of your staff. You need to impose deadlines, but accounting for every moment of someone's work and time can lead to pressure for that person, as can a lack of structure. If people do not know what you expect of them, or when you expect it by, this frustrates the need for structure. Exercise 8.5 is designed to help you consider the ways this need can be frustrated in your organization and what you can do to alleviate the frustration.

Satisfaction of the three basic needs is crucial for well-being and good performance. Within the organization, whether through its policies, systems or structures; there can be too little recognition or too much of the wrong kind; too little variety or an excess of stimulation; too little structure or not enough stability. Whether originating in the organization, the working of teams or you as a manager, any actions which frustrate these needs will lead to unnecessary and inappropriate pressure. Pressure is inappropriate when it hinders optimum performance and unnecessary when it is not related to the objectives of the organization.

Reducing the causes of inappropriate pressure on staff means recognizing the effects on them of your expectations and your behaviour, and how needs can be frustrated at work. Organizational life brings enough pressure in itself, without adding unnecessary or inappropriate pressure. Reducing these pressures is an important part of the organizational survival guide.

Exercises for Chapter 8: How you can reduce unnecessary pressure in your organization

Exercise 8.1 You as a mammoth for others: Are you a 'busy' manager?

You can be a mammoth to your staff through your own style of working. Decide whether the following statements are always true, sometimes true or never true about the way you behave at work.

	Always	Sometimes	Never
1. I always walk quickly rather than slowly.			
2. It matters to me that I am seen to do better than other people.			
3. I need to feel that I am the best.			
4. I often do half a dozen things at once.			
5. I rarely concentrate solely on one thing at a time.			
6. I know where I am going and nothing is going to stop me.			
7. I do not suffer fools gladly.			
8. I work better when the deadline for the task is imminent.			
9. I like to have a sense of challenge in my work.			
10. I battle on against all odds.			
11. I make decisions quickly and rarely need a lot of thought.			
12. My communication is concise and to the point.			
13. In my view people around me take too long to complete tasks.			
14. Jobs always seem to take longer than I expect.			
15. I always work longer than normal office hours.			

The way in which you answered these questions will give you a clearer idea of whether or not you are prone to 'busyness'.

If most of your responses fell into the 'always' column you are not only constantly putting pressure on yourself; you will be a definite source of pressure for others.

If most of your responses fell into the 'sometimes' column, you will still be putting pressure on yourself and others, but it will be less consistent. Reflect for yourself on the situations in which you are drawn into these patterns of behaviour.

If most of your responses fell into the 'never' column you will be less prone to 'busyness' and, while not exempt from pressure, you are probaby not pressuring yourself or others too much in this way.

Exercise 8.2: How values and expectations can cause pressure in the organization

In this exercise we suggest you consider the values which operate in your work team and in the organization as a whole.

The expectations of the work team

We want you to focus on the teams or groups of which you are a member. Complete the following statements about each group you are involved with to get a clear idea of the expectations the group has of its members.

In this group a member is expected to:

In this group discussion focuses on:

In this group business is conducted:

In this group the formal leader:

In this group tension is:

In this group disagreement is:

In this group relationships are expected to be:

In this group the style of working is:

In this group the most important thing is:

In this group (fill in any other expectations you can identify):

Now answer the question: What pressure do these expectations place on group members?

Reflect on the pressures you have identified and note those which in your estimation are unnecessary and inappropriate.

Unnecessary or inappropriate pressures in this team are:

What can you do to reduce them?

The values of the organization

Now transfer your attention to the organization as a whole. Complete the following statements about your organization.

In this organization a good boss:

In this organization a good member of staff:

In this organization what matters most is:

In this organization what matters least is:

In this organization praise is given for:

In this organization criticism is given for:

In this organization people are expected to work in this way:

In this organization people are expected not to work in this way:

In this organization (fill in any other values you can identify):

Now answer the question: What pressures do these values and beliefs place on organizational members?

Identify those which are unnecessary or inappropriate:

What can you do to reduce them?

Exercise 8.3 *How does the organization frustrate the need for recognition?*

When the need for recognition and contact is not met within an organization, frustration and stress frequently occur. Decide whether the following statements are rarely true, sometimes true or always true about your organization, to gain a clearer idea of whether it frustrates this need.

Rarely   Sometimes   Always

1. Individual achievement is recognized by the organization.
2. Recognition is given for the work of a team or group.
3. Promotion is based on merit rather than other factors such as length of service.
4. There is concern shown for the career needs of staff.
5. The salary structure includes reward for merit and achievement.
6. There are jobs which isolate people.
7. There is a formal, impersonal climate.
8. There is a great deal of stereotyping in the organization.
9. There are jobs which involve frequent impersonal dealings with others.
10. The disciplinary procedure is detailed compared with any congratulatory system.

Scoring

Score 2 points for every time you marked 'always' in response to questions 1–5. Score 1 point for every time you marked 'sometimes' in response to question 1–5. Score 2 points for every time you marked 'rarely' in response to questions 6–10. Score 1 point for every time you marked 'sometimes' in response to questions 6–10.

If you scored *between 0 and 10* it is likely that the need for recognition and contact is frustrated in your organization. If you scored *between 11 and 20* it is less likely that there will be frustration due to lack of recognition.

Are there any steps you need to take to improve recognition and contact satisfaction?

Exercise 8.4 *How does the organization frustrate the need for variety and stimulation?*

Everyone needs a certain amount of variety and stimulation to perform at their best. If this need is not met, people will experience frustration. Decide whether the following statements are always true, sometimes true or never true about your organization, to gain a clearer idea of whether it causes unnecessary pressure in this way.

	Always	*Sometimes*	*Never*
1. Attention is paid in the organization to providing variety at work.			
2. Steps are taken to ensure that each job is stimulating.			
3. This organization strives to ensure that meetings are not tedious.			
4. Challenge at work is important in this organization.			
5. Jobs are designed to keep routine work at an appropriate level.			
6. There are few jobs which are largely repetitive.			
7. We try to ensure that no one is overloaded with work.			
8. There are plenty of new ideas in this organization.			
9. This organization encourages creativity and innovation.			
10. The organization is not bound by rigid rules.			

If you answered 'yes' to most of the statements, it is likely that the organization takes account of the need for variety and stimulation. If you answered 'no' to most of the questions, you may well find frustration in the organization. If your answers fell into the 'sometimes' column, identify specific jobs which need your attention.

What steps can you take to bring variety and stimulation to an optimum level in your department or organization?

Exercise 8.5 How does the organization frustrate the need for stability and structure?

We all need some structure and stability in our lives at work. Lack of stability or too much structure can cause frustration. Decide whether the following statements are always true, sometimes true or never true about your organization, to gain a clearer idea of whether it causes frustration in this way.

Always   Sometimes   Never

1. Each member of staff has a lot of freedom to determine his or her own workload.
2. Each member of staff has a choice over what work he or she does.
3. There are few hard-and-fast rules in this organization.
4. Everyone knows what is expected of him or her.
5. Everyone knows the strategy and direction of the organization.
6. Generally speaking people are not subject to conflicting expectations and demands.
7. Organizational restructuring is only carried out when appropriate, not as a management panacea for unresolved problems.
8. Whenever there is a change in the organization, steps are taken to ensure a smooth transition.
9. There is a lot of preparation for organizational change which involves the staff.
10. The effects of change are taken into account.

If you mainly marked 'sometimes' or 'never' in response to the questions, there is a high possibility that your organization is frustrating the need for structure and stability. If you mainly marked 'always' it is less likely that your organization is frustrating this need.

Are there any areas in which you need to take action?

9. Making the organization fitter to cope and perform well

The final elements in the organizational survival guide are the various ways in which you can make your organization fitter to cope with the pressures it faces. Optimum performance needs optimum pressure, which means a match between the demands and challenges facing the organization and the ability to meet those demands. We have already considered the skills you need as a manager to help staff when pressure affects them, and how an organization can put unnecessary pressure on its members. In this chapter we explore the ways in which you can increase the organization's ability to cope with pressure.

This is a long-term strategy and means paying attention to each of the three levels of the organizational system. You can take steps to make individual members of staff fitter to cope with pressure, to help teams to develop more constructive ways of working together, and to increase the capacity of the organization, or your part of it, by reviewing its design and climate. Fit individuals can grow and adapt to changes which affect them at work; fit teams perform well and can accommodate pressure and change more easily than groups which struggle together; and a fit organization has a value system which is capable of guiding it through difficult times and a design which helps rather than hinders its aims and purpose.

Helping your staff get fitter to deal with pressure

Performance at work depends on three elements: the individual's capacity or ability; his or her inclination or motivation to do the job; and the opportunity the job provides for the individual to use his or her skills. To take an example from outside the work setting, in order to play a piano you need skills, technical ability and the desire to play, and you must have access to a piano. In the work setting there is little point in equipping staff with a set of skills if there is no opportunity — and no prospect of opportunity — for using those skills. Equally one cannot expect people to perform a job well if they have neither the necessary skills nor the inclination.

Making staff fitter to cope with pressure involves balancing the skill, inclination and opportunities presented within the organization. People doing jobs for which they are well equipped in terms of skills and inclination are less likely to perceive threats and succumb to modern-day mammoths. To enable an individual to balance these elements you as a manager need to pay attention to three areas. First of all you need to be clear what expectations you have of each person and to convey this clearly to the individual. Second, you need to ensure that each individual has feedback on his or her performance. Staff development or appraisal schemes are ways in which this can be achieved. Finally, you need to develop the skills of your staff. This can either by done off the job by training programmes or on the job by, for example, coaching.

Clarifying the expectations placed on your staff

Each person within an organization has a particular role to fulfil. Each job carries certain expectations. A salesperson is expected to reach sales targets, an accountant to provide financial information, a manager to run a department or section. This seems straightforward enough, but in practice two problems can arise. First, the individual may not be clear what his or her allotted task involves. This is particularly so as people rise through the hierarchy and become less directly involved at the sharp end of the organization's work. Assembly-line workers may be clear that the job involves, for example, placing nuts on each wheel as it passes in front of them; when promoted to supervisor, they may be less clear what the job entails. Similarly, social workers may be clear that the job involves handling particular cases which their professional training has equipped them to handle, but may be less clear about their role if they are promoted to team leader. Job descriptions, however well written, rarely overcome this problem. Many commonly used terms, such as 'responsible for the work of . . . ', do not always clarify the position. Ambiguity therefore can occur when the person in the job is not clear precisely what the job entails.

A second problem can arise if an individual is not clear about the amount of work he or she is required to do. How many cases is a social worker expected to take on, for example; and how many nuts is the assembly-line worker expected to screw on per hour? This ambiguity often causes pressure, as does any lack of clarity about the level of performance expected. We all need to know both *what* we are expected to do and also *how much* of it is required.

Ambiguity can be exacerbated when an individual is subject to conflicting expectations. As very few people work in isolation most jobs relate to the work of others. Each person the postholder deals with will have his or her own expectations of the performance of that person. These are more likely to be expectations of behaviour or style than quantitative expectations. People may be clear what the organization expects of them, but unable to act in a way which satisfies conflicting demands from others. The role of a middle manager has been described as that of a pig-in-the-middle, sandwiched between the expectations of staff and those of senior management, and hemmed in by the expectations of colleagues. In this case ambiguity is less likely to be a problem than conflicting expectations.

Conflicting expectations can occur within the job and also between the various roles each person fills. Within a job conflicting expectations can be generated by different people the job-holder deals with. For example, you may expect a member of your staff to attend a number of regular meetings as your deputy; meanwhile the individual's colleagues expect him or her to be behind his or her desk to answer their queries; and your customers want the same individual to be out visiting them on their sites. Your member of staff cannot be everywhere simultaneously, and you need to work with the person to balance these conflicting expectations. An example of conflict between roles is where a job requires travel away from home which conflicts with the family's expectations. Many people attempt to overcome conflicting demands on their time between home and work by taking work home.

Conflicts either within a single role or between roles can be resolved. The first step is to examine with the person concerned the whole set of expectations experienced. Negotiation and agreement is then possible; priorities can be clarified and these can be communicated to all those who need to know. You can help in this process by specifying what is required from each member of staff and ensuring that this is understood. Where there is ambiguity or conflict between the various people with whom a member of staff interacts, systematic analysis and clarification of the demands can go a long way to resolving problems. This frequently needs to be done by all members of a section or department together, although it can be undertaken just with the individual concerned. The key element is that you initiate discussion about the expectations of the organization and other people.

Clarifying expectations through analysis of each role in the organization fulfils two functions. It enables each person to be clear about what is expected of him or her, which understanding then forms the basis of his or her actions at work. Additionally it removes pressure caused by the ambiguity or conflict experienced in the role. Exercise 9.1 at the end of this chapter helps you to clarify expectations with your staff.

Knowledge about what is required or expected is thus an important aspect of good performance, but in itself will not make individuals fitter to cope with pressure. Feedback on performance is also needed.

Giving feedback to your staff

When people know what is expected of them they can form their own assessments of whether they are meeting requirements. However, as a manager you also need to provide feedback on performance. People need information on their past performance in order to make decisions about future actions and how to improve their performance. Knowledge of what is expected will give information about the skills and behaviours required in a post, but it does not provide information about whether those skills and behaviours have actually been used. You can provide this information through an appraisal or staff-development scheme, whether or not there is an organization-wide system. You need a systematic approach to providing the feedback each person needs. This is part of the process of enabling people to do their jobs well and so helps them become fitter to cope with pressure.

Appraisal and staff-development schemes are characterized by regular interviews between a manager and each of his or her staff. During the course of the interview the manager provides information on the performance of the member of staff. The feedback offered relates specifically to the performance of the individual against standards previously agreed. The person being interviewed offers his or her own view of his or her performance, the problems encountered and the assistance required. This is then used as a basis for joint discussion. Finally agreement is reached about future action. The goals for the coming period and steps to be taken by you or by your member of staff to improve or maintain performance are set.

Unfortunately in many instances an appraisal interview is seen by both manager and staff as an occasion when weaknesses are highlighted. The interviews can be modern-day mammoths for both parties as few people relish having their mistakes emphasized, and many managers recoil from the prospect of having to list the misdeeds of a person to his or her face. A properly handled appraisal or staff-development interview should incorporate positive feedback. Providing only negative feedback is uncomfortable for both parties, and can be unproductive. Everyone needs to know how well they have performed as well as the areas where, in the organization's view, they have not performed so well. Feedback needs to be balanced.

Information about past performance needs to be specific if it is to be useful. Satisfying as it might be to hear that you have done a wonderful job over the past year, it is more helpful to know how this view has been formed. Negative feedback, in particular, needs to be related to particular events. Simply to learn that your manager is not happy with your performance is difficult enough but is also too vague to be useful.

A staff-development interview is an opportunity for you to gain a greater understanding of why staff perform as they do. It may uncover a mismatch between the individual's skills and inclination and the demands of the job. Motivation is greatly enhanced by the time and care you take to give feedback at regular intervals and to explore the reason for any discrepancy between expectations and performance.

Appraisal and staff-development schemes are formal ways in which an organization recognizes the need for feedback and uses it as a basis for decisions about future performance. Even if the organization does not operate a formal scheme, giving regular and detailed feedback on performance is still one of the main ways in which you can make your staff fitter to cope with the pressures they face. By giving feedback and listening to staff you can exchange useful information, and often both enhance the confidence of your staff and meet their need for recognition. It does, however, need to be done skilfully and assertively. We discussed the skill of assertion in Chapter 4 and Table 4.3 outlined some hints for giving praise and criticism assertively. Table 9.1 shows the main points to be aware of when giving constructive feedback. Exercise 9.2 at the end of the chapter helps you prepare constructive feedback for your staff.

Feedback is generally most helpful where:
 – It concentrates on things which the receiver can do something about.
 – It is as specific as possible.
 – Understanding is checked.
 – It comments on things done well as well as things which need improvement.
 – The 'receiver' is listened to.

Table 9.1 Giving effective feedback on performance

During an appraisal or development interview you will also identify any need for development in the skills of your staff. Developing the skills of your staff is the next way in which you can develop their fitness for coping with pressure.

Developing the skills of your staff

Development of the skills of your staff to cope with the pressures they face can take two forms. First, you can foster the development of a personal survival guide by encouraging each person to follow the principles and techniques we outlined in Part 1. This incorporates identifying how they create unnecessary pressure for themselves, developing their assertive skills and taking steps to reduce wear and tear on their systems.

Second, you can make your staff fitter to cope with pressure by developing the skills they need to perform their jobs. These may be technical or social skills. If people are not equipped with the capacities necessary to do a task, no amount of motivation or opportunity will lead to good performance. Instead they will experience pressure. Being faced with situations or tasks you are not equipped to deal with because you lack the necessary knowledge or skills leads to low self-confidence. When self-confidence is low, you are more prone to perceive modern-day mammoths. Enhancing self-confidence so that it incorporates a realistic expectation of success will help staff become fitter to deal with pressure. This can be achieved in two ways: off-the-job training and on-the-job coaching.

Training: Increasing skills and confidence off the job

The aim of training is to increase the capacity of staff to do the job they currently undertake or to prepare them for new responsibilities and tasks. It can increase knowledge or improve skills. In either case training needs to be linked closely to the needs of the organization and the demands of the job. Providing staff with knowledge or skills they have little opportunity to use will not enhance performance, and may lead to frustration. Decisions as to how to use training, whom to train and what in, need to be made on the basis of information about each person. Analysis of training needs is a prerequisite for effective use of development activities.

Knowledge-based development can take various forms, but it typically involves attendance at a course or conference designed to impart information about particular topics. Information technology, social change, product developments and legal issues are examples of areas where knowledge is imparted in this way, though one can of course keep up with professional developments and research findings by reading relevant journals as well. The aim is to increase the knowledge people have about a topic; this form of development will not necessarily enhance their ability to use the knowledge acquired.

Skills-based development, on the other hand, aims to train people to become more proficient in the use of certain behaviours. Assertiveness training, for example, is designed to increase the incidence of assertive behaviours. Training in selling techniques focuses on the behaviour needed to sell a product successfully. In all skill development new knowledge is necessary. You need to know what assertiveness means before you can become skilled at asserting yourself, just as you need to identify the behaviours associated with successful selling before you can become skilled at it. However, the aim of skills training is to incorporate the three elements of knowledge, observation and practice to alter subsequent *actions*.

Training and development activities are very powerful ways of improving the fitness of staff to cope with pressure, but there are a number of conditions attached to their successful use. First, the training needs to be suitable for and needed by the individual; second, any view of training as a reward or punishment needs to be discouraged; and third, preparation is usually needed if staff are to get optimum value out of a training activity. You as a manager have an important role to play in this last area, as well as in helping staff to make best use of their training after it is completed.

The value of training is often lost because the member of staff is not involved in the decision to give him or her the training, and is not prepared for it. As training takes place away from the job, the links between the training and work activities need to be clear and discussed jointly. A problem can also occur when a member of staff returns from a course only to be greeted with humorous comments about holidays, or if the training he or she has received is simply ignored. Debriefing staff and discussing the ways in which the training can be applied in the job are vital factors affecting its success. Training away from the job can be a powerful development technique because distractions are few, and an environment of trust and experimentation can be created quickly, so that the experience can be intense. It needs to be integrated with day-to-day work carefully. This is less of a problem with an alternative approach to developing staff — coaching on the job.

Coaching: Increasing skills and confidence on the job

'Coaching' is a term typically associated with sporting activities but it can also form a very useful part of the organizational survival guide. When you take the time to coach staff, you increase both their skills and their confidence.

Coaching is an activity whereby you help someone to perform a task better than he or she could have done otherwise. The medium for coaching is discussion between you and the member of staff. It consists of three elements: talking through a particular task, observing performance, and jointly discussing its outcome. Consider this process in terms of coaching in a sport, such as tennis. The coach discusses with the learner what makes a good forehand drive, watches him or her in action and then discusses the performance. Coaching at work follows the same lines. Table 9.2 outlines the coaching process, which relies on discussion, rather than simply telling a person what to do. Coaching develops skill and confidence by using many of the skills identified in Chapter 7 as useful in a helping interview. It also involves the use of skilled feedback, aimed at encouraging the individual.

- Recognize/make an opportunity for development.
- Through discussion, agree a plan.
- Set goals for development.
- Provide/ensure opportunities to practise.
- Plan review of progress.
- Jointly assess development.
- Identify further development needs.

Table 9.2 The coaching process

Any aspect of work can be suitable for coaching. It can relate to an individual's day-to-day job or a special project or secondment. A coaching session need not be a formal interview. The one element it does require is time, but time spent with staff in this way is time well spent. Exercise 9.3 focuses on the planning of training and coaching for staff.

You can improve the fitness of staff to deal with pressure by clarifying expectations, by appraisal and development to ensure regular feedback, and by developing skills and knowledge. You have an important part to play in these activities. However, increasing an organization's fitness to cope with pressure means paying attention to more than individual members of staff, their abilities, motivation and opportunities; it also means developing the work of teams within your part of the organization.

Helping groups get fitter to deal with pressure

The first step you can take to make a team fitter to cope with pressure is to be aware of the attributes of a fit team so that you know what you are aiming for. A team which is working well will be able to withstand a higher level of pressure. A group of people who meet occasionally but who do not pull together to achieve good results is not a team. Developing a real team requires commitment from all the members to improve ways of working and relationships so that better results are obtained.

What makes a team fit?

The characteristics of a fit team relate to the way it works together to meets its objectives and to the relationships between members. A successful team achieves its aims and is productive, and there are good working relationships between its members and between the team and the rest of the organization. The four primary attributes of a fit team can be summarized as:

- Sound mechanisms for working.
- Effective leadership.
- Good interpersonal relationships.
- Good relationships with the rest of the organization.

A team which is not clear about its tasks, or about whether topics are for discussion or decision, will not work well. Each member needs to know the agenda, however informal it may be, and to prepare for the meeting. In unfit teams the 'real' agenda is not known to all members even if a formal agenda listing the items for discussion has been circulated. In an unfit team the issues are never clarified for everyone. Problems within the group never surface, and so are not discussed and resolved. People need to understand why they are meeting. When there is lack of clarity or consensus as to the purpose of the group, commitment will be less than if there is full knowledge and agreement of objectives. The team needs to have sound methods for handling discussion, for agreeing how meetings will be organized, and for achieving specific tasks. The method by which the agenda for meetings is drawn up is also important. If it is compiled by one person, he or she will dominate. This can lead to problems in the second main area of difference between fit and unfit teams — how leadership is exercised within the group.

A fit team has effective leadership. Leadership means having a sense of purpose and taking action to ensure that the team meets its objectives. Unfortunately leadership is often taken to relate only to the formal leader, and is frequently confused with chairing meetings. Most working groups include one person who by virtue of seniority, expertise or appointment is attributed the formal leader role. As many groups have discovered, leaving leadership to the formal leader alone hinders rather than helps group working. Leadership needs rather to be shared between team members so that each person is committed to the purpose of the group and takes steps to steer the group in the direction indicated by the purpose.

Leadership also involves the management of relations within the team. Responsibility for this aspect of group working is less tangible but also needs to be shared between members; if each member does not contribute to it valuable information or opinion can be lost. To leave the responsibility for the management of relations to the formal leader is to place an undue burden on one individual. It is unrealistic to expect one person to steer the team and to manage its relationships alone. Effective leadership within a group occurs when members take responsibility for the work of the group. Achieving goals will be more likely if leadership is exercised so as to take account both of the tasks of the team and the needs of its members.

The management of relationships within the group will determine whether a team is fit or not. There are three main characteristics of good interpersonal relationships within a team:

- Trust and openness.
- Cooperation.
- Effective handling of disagreements.

An unfit group is characterized by a low level of sharing of information, feelings and opinions, because of inhibitions about possible responses. If a member of a group expects scorn or hostility, for example, from the other members, he or she will be less willing to volunteer a view. Cooperation is needed to pull together the contributions of the members, who may well come from different professional disciplines and different parts of the organization. A management team, for example, which is seen as a battlefield by its members will face more modern-day mammoths than should be the case. If members of a group expect the meetings to be characterized by competition they will go to the meetings 'armed', which will increase the incidence of aggressive, unassertive and passive behaviours.

Even where groups operate according to the belief that disagreement between members is undesirable, there will be many occasions on which differences occur between people working together. How these differences are handled will distinguish a fit from an unfit group. If any disagreement is seen as conflict, and potentially harmful or threatening to the group, group members will suppress any discord and the group will be characterized less by consensus and more by compliance. This is an unassertive way of handling a modern-day mammoth. If on the other hand differences between group members are seen as useful opportunities for getting information about the views and feelings of people in the group and talking through the issue until consensus is reached, this will lead to a greater sense of commitment to the team as well as to its decisions.

The final area where fit and unfit groups differ is in their relationships with other groups and the rest of the organization. Again, a battlefield approach will lead to relations between the group and the rest of the system deteriorating. Much group time can be wasted on waging war on outside groups. A fit team takes account of the rest of the organization, identifies the groups whose work impinges on its work, and manages its external relationships in such a way that little competition or hostility develops. In this way the organization gets the best results as well. Unfortunately the siege mentality which can develop if a group feels threatened by outsiders can act to pull the group members together and can occasionally be used to inculcate a spurious sense of harmony and togetherness in the group.

Recognizing the differences between a fit and an unfit group is the first step you can take to develop team fitness. The next step is using this information.

How to develop a fit team

Developing a fit team takes time. A newly formed group will work differently from a team which has been working together for a long time, but it should not be assumed that a group which has been working together for a while has grown fitter as time has passed. A long-standing group will have established ways of working together, but these will not always be constructive. After a time together a group may be characterized by a low level of trust, competitive exchanges between members, a lack of concern with its objectives, and suppression of conflict. This is an unfit group. A group may improve its fitness over time, but developing a fit team means more than prolonging the life of a group in the hope that it will become fitter.

Developing a fit team involves three stages: assessment of the group; open review of its working; and decisions about future working. These three stages involve consideration of how the group works as well as what it does. Assessment needs to be made of the processes which occur in a group as well as of the content of its discussions and the tasks it undertakes. A fit team is more likely to incorporate attention to the way it works into its normal procedures and to view this as necessary to group success. An unfit group is unlikely to pay regular attention to reviewing its progress.

While a fit team can incorporate review into its normal activities, it is a common practise to set aside time purely for review. Frequently this takes the form of a team-building workshop. The team allocates a period of time, often two to three days, away from the office to assess itself, review the situation and make decisions about its future. If the review takes this form it is also common practise to involve an outside consultant to assist the process. This is a good idea as it is then possible for the formal leader to become part of the team rather than acting as the manager of the review. Usually the formal leader instigates the process and then calls on the expertise of an experienced outsider to manage the process. Table 9.3 gives some guidelines about when it is useful to use an external consultant to help team development.

- To help start up.
- When the team does not have the skills both to manage and to take part in team-development activities.
- When there are sensitive issues to work through.
- When the team manager feels too involved to stand back.
- To give impartial feedback.
- To help review progress.
- To help with intergroup problems which are difficult for the team to manage alone.

Table 9.3 When to use an external consultant to help team development

You can assess a team's current fitness by using questionnaires to gain information, through discussion or through observation. The aim is to establish a picture of the team as it currently operates. It is advisable to gain as much information from as many sources as possible; this includes the views of the group members themselves. There is not likely to be universal agreement about the current state of the group and care needs to be taken at this stage to gain a representative picture.

The second stage in developing a fit team, the review, calls for an evaluation of the information gleaned in the first stage, with the aim of identifying areas for future decisions. At this stage an agenda for change is drawn up which takes the group, by way of much discussion and exchange of views, into the final stage.

The final stage of developing a fit team is the decision-taking stage when measures to correct problems are discussed. This stage can take a considerable time as there needs to be consensus on the decisions taken. This is the time not to suppress differences but to explore them fully.

Developing team fitness, therefore, means devoting time and effort to assessment and review of how the group works. The final stage — planning ahead — will lead to further monitoring of the changes decided upon. Eventually, such monitoring will become a normal part of a fit team's working pattern. As a team increases its fitness, it will increase the care it takes over assessing itself, while paradoxically needing such assessment less; but even fit teams need to incorporate regular review into their agenda. By taking time to monitor its strengths and weaknesses, whether or not it involves an outside consultant, a team will become fitter to cope with pressure and less prone to stress.

As a manager your role in developing a fit team is to:
- Assess whether a team needs developing to make it fitter.
- Set the climate for review by talking to the group and individuals about the problems facing the group.
- Organize a review period, bringing in an outside consultant when necessary.

Exercise 9.4 is designed to help you start on the process of developing a fit team.

Helping the organization get fitter to deal with pressure

A fit organization which can deal effectively with the pressures it faces is above all an organization which is adaptable and flexible. We argued earlier against the policy of using organizational restructuring as the initial response to problems, but that does not mean we are arguing for organizational ossification. Change in any of the demands facing an organization, whether the change originates from outside or from within, requires adaptability. A fit organization develops the ability to be flexible. The key is being able to adapt to inevitable change, rather than using change as a customary response to problems and pressure.

To draw an analogy with personal physical fitness, an organization needs strength, suppleness and above all stamina. The strength of an organization lies in its resources; it needs suppleness to bend and be flexible; it needs stamina to keep going. The heart of an organization is its culture and style, which provide the driving force for its work, but a good heart is little use without strength in the rest of the body, which is provided by the design of the organization.

Organizational culture: The heart at work

The culture of the organization is the sum of the core values characterizing it. These core values inform all aspects of organizational life, as the heart influences the whole body. An unfit organization has values which are not clear to the members of the organization, or are inappropriate for the work of the organization. A difficult, but important, role for you as a manager is to influence the values which shape the work of your department.

The values of an organization are reflected in its design and structure. For example, an organization which holds the view that its staff matter and are responsible people will not design meaningless and routine jobs nor impose a many-tiered system of control. An organization which holds the value that customers and clients matter will demonstrate this through its reception area, the way 'phone callers are dealt with, and the care it devotes to its dealings with customers. When you are clear what values are important in your part of the organization you can begin to ensure that they are reflected in 'the way things get done around here'.

The culture of an organization is apparent in many ways. For example, it can be seen in the titles given to staff, the myths people have about the organization, the style of its training, facilities such as the canteen, and the things people believe they are rewarded for.

The culture can often be summed up in the phrases which express the key values dominant in the organization, e.g., value for money or quality of service. The values can be implicit or explicitly stated. Often they grow up with the organization; the values of the founder, for example, can be passed on through the organization for many years and inform its way of working. One of your tasks as a manager is to ensure that each member of staff acts in accordance with the key values and expectations of the organization. When values are explicitly articulated, they become part of management thinking and are embodied in the induction, training and evaluation of people's work. Organizations where the values are clear to all are likely to have slogans, mottoes or symbols with which everyone can identify and which inform everyday behaviour. For the organization to change or clarify its values a concerted approach from senior managers is required, which needs to permeate every part of the organization. The key values need to embody the mission of the organization so that members know what business they are in and therefore what they are aiming for in their jobs. For example, a public-sector organization whose key value is 'excellence of service for the public' and which articulates this clearly to all its staff and incorporates it into all its activity will be a very different place to work in and receive services from than one whose key value is 'adequate low-cost service' (even if this is not explicitly stated).

As a manager you need to clarify your values and those prevailing in the organization. You need to make explicit statements of the values which you believe should inform people's work. You need to ensure that the way you do things in your department reflects those beliefs and values.

Whatever the culture of the organization, whether or not it hinders effective working will depend on whether the values are appropriate. Whether the culture is appropriate will depend on its compatibility with the organization's aims, objectives and strategy.

Organizational design: Getting the body of work done

The design of an organization reflects its culture and, viewed in isolation, with no reference to culture, it becomes an empty shell. No amount of attention to organizational design will compensate for a lack of direction or lack of driving force. Alternatively a clear sense of purpose needs an organization fit to follow the chosen path.

To ensure a fit organization, you need to devote attention to three aspects of organizational design: how the work is differentiated, how it is integrated, and the systems and processes which facilitate it.

Differentiation of work and job design

To achieve its purpose an organization needs to break its work down into component parts, designing jobs to be performed by different members of staff. The larger an organization grows the more complex will be the process of job design. However, there are some general issues which a fit organization addresses. First, tasks need to be identified and then grouped together. Second, the content of each job description is scrutinized for its relation to overall goals as well as for the extent to which it meets the needs of individuals. It can be easy to design a job which is economic of effort, but which is so routine and repetitive that it de-skills those expected to do it.

Integration of work: The hierarchy

Once work has been differentiated and the division of labour identified, the organization then faces the problem of integrating and coordinating the separate jobs. It does this through its structure, in particular through the hierarchy of different levels. There is no single best structure; it depends on what the structure is expected to do. The shape of the hierarchy will depend on the nature of the tasks as well as the strategy of the organization. Some organizations need a flat structure with few levels of management, which allows and demands a relatively large degree of autonomy; others need a narrow tall structure. As well as taking account of the need to coordinate activities, the structure of a fit organization reflects the organization's key values.

Systems and processes: Making it work

There are three main systems within the body of the organization which a fit organization provides for. First, there is a need for an explicit system whereby information is collected and distributed to where it is needed. In particular, the information needed for financial control must be supplied. Second, the system of reward needs careful consideration, not only because it will affect individual performance, but also because reward systems are the main way an organization gives recognition to staff. The third system needing particular attention is the system for recruitment and promotion, by which an organization fits people to jobs. Not only does a fit organization need fit staff; it needs each of its staff to be in the right job. This means considering the psychological needs of staff as well as whether they have the necessary skills and technical ability.

Information, reward and recruitment systems are the lubricators which facilitate the process of differentiation and integration. All these factors need to be taken into account if an organization is to be fit for the pressures it faces and adaptable. Stress can occur in an organization which has inappropriate differentiation and integration. This can be exacerbated if its financial and other control systems are also inadequate and inappropriate.

For example, an organization in which the jobs are made up of easily specified routine tasks can have a clear hierarchical control system in which similar jobs are grouped together and report directly to one person. The span of control of that person is limited largely by the number of people doing the same kind of work. Standardized systems can be used in such an organization. This kind of design would lead to considerable pressure in an organization which cannot specify jobs so closely. Where the tasks are complex, the organization is best served by ensuring that its members are professionally trained and capable of self-regulation. The hierarchy then deals with exceptions and problems rather than controlling precisely the work of all staff.

Tensions often occur in organizations which require *both* kinds of tasks — the routine and the complex — to be done. The organization then has to resolve the difficulties encountered when some staff require the control systems, information systems and lack of hierarchical emphasis suited to trained professionals while other staff are working in a closely specified and structured environment.

In their pure forms, neither of these kinds of organizational design works very well when quick change is needed. Professional organizations can be slow to adapt, as people become attached to the professional values and ethos which are so important for self-regulating behaviour. Similarly, when every detail is specified and rule-bound, organizations are slow to uproot. Organizations can cope with this by creating small teams whose remit is to create and adapt to new opportunities and overcome problems. The teams are not rule bound or single-profession based and work on an egalitarian basis in which the achievements of the team act as an incentive and source of satisfaction. This kind of structure can be a great source of energy helping otherwise static organizations to adapt to changes.

While you may not be able to influence the design of the whole organization you can look at the design of jobs and structures in your own department. You can look at your personnel practises and review whether you need to change them. Exercise 9.5 at the end of this chapter helps you think through the fitness of your organization. By comparing your organization with a really unfit one you can assess how unfit yours is and what needs changing.

Exercises for Chapter 9: Getting the organization fitter to cope with pressure

Exercise 9.1 Clarifying expectations in the organization: Are there any problems?

The first stage in analysing and clarifying roles is to check whether each member of staff has a clear understanding of the expectations of the organization. A useful way of starting to do this is to look at the use of job descriptions. Consider the following questions.

1. Does each person have a job description?
2. Is each job description clear and specific in the tasks it outlines?
3. Does each person understand his or her job description?
4. If there is any lack of clarity or misunderstanding, what steps can be taken to specify the expectations of the organization?

Each person in the organization interacts with others in the course of his or her work. Even if the job as defined by the organization is clear, problems can still arise through the conflicting expectations of others.

We suggest that this exercise is undertaken by a work group together, although it can be of benefit when done by one individual.

Step 1: Drawing a role map

Each person should start by identifying the people he or she has contact with in the course of work. These should be noted on a role map, as shown below.

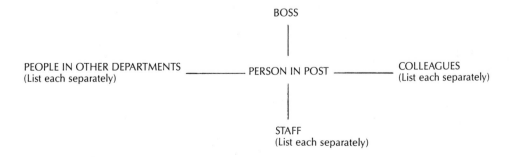

Step 2: Identifying expectations

Once each person has drawn a role map, the next stage is to identify the expectations the people listed on a role map have of the post-holder at its centre.

Each person is asked to list the expectations which he or she *thinks are held* by the others on his or her role map. Mark these on the role map.

Step 3: Clarifying expectations

Discussion of the expectations listed is the next stage. Two problems can occur.

- The post-holder is not clear what expectations another person has of him or her — there is ambiguity.
- The expectations are conflicting.

The post-holder can clarify expectations by discussion with those who make up his or her role map. Conflict can occur when two people expect different things of the post-holder, but discussion amongst all those involved can resolve the problem. Alternatively, one person may have conflicting expectations of the post-holder; discussion can resolve this as well.

Prepare yourself for a discussion aimed at resolving ambiguity about what others expect of you by answering the following questions:

1. Do you experience any ambiguity in your job?

2. What are you not clear about?

3. Who can give you the information you need?

4. How can you initiate discussion to get information?

Prepare yourself for a discussion aimed at resolving conflicting expectations held by others about your job by answering the following questions:

1. Do you experience conflicting expectations?

2. Where does the conflict lie?

3. How can you initiate discussion to resolve conflict?

Exercise 9.2 Developing staff: Planning to give feedback

Whether or not your organization has a formal appraisal scheme or a system of staff-development interviews, it is important to incorporate giving feedback into your managerial role. This exercise aims to help you plan to give feedback to members of your staff.

Consider each member of your staff in turn, working through the questions below.

1. What are the main areas of responsibility facing the member of staff you are considering?

Now decide on the period of time you want to consider. Focus on the individual's performance of his or her prime tasks over that period.

2. What aspects of his or her performance were you pleased with? Be as specific as you can.

3. What aspects of his or her performance were you not pleased with? Again, be as specific as you can.

4. Do you have sufficient information about his or her performance? If not, what information do you need?

5. How can you get the necessary information?

6. How do other people view the performance of this person?

7. Pulling together all the information available on this person's performance, are the aspects you are less happy with open to change, and can the person do something about them?

Aspects of performance you wish to change	Open to change	Not open to change
(a)		
(b)		
(c)		
(d)		
(e)		

Now consider Table 9.1 which outlines the features of constructive feedback. Plan how you are going to give feedback, remembering to incorporate positive comments on good performance as well as focusing on aspects you are not happy with.

Positive aspects I want to comment on	How I plan to do it
(a)	
(b)	
(c)	
(d)	
(e)	

Aspects I am not happy about	How I plan to give this feedback
(a)	
(b)	
(c)	
(d)	
(e)	

Choose or create a suitable occasion to give this feedback. If this form of feedback is unfamiliar to your staff you will need to set the scene, explaining why you believe a performance review and information about how they are doing is important. Remember that in an exchange they may have useful information for you too. Listening is as important as telling.

Excercise 9.3 Developing staff: Planning training and coaching

What knowledge and skills are needed?

Developing staff will increase their ability to do their jobs and help them withstand pressure. Development needs to be linked to the needs of the organization as well as the needs of the individual.

Focus on the staff you are responsible for and identify the knowledge and skills they need to do their jobs. Then reflect on whether they have the necessary knowledge and skills.

	Knowledge needed for job		*Skills needed for job*		*Discrepancies*
Staff member	Knowledge needed	Does individual have required knowledge?	Skills needed	Does individual have required skill?	Areas for development

1.

2.

3.

Areas for development: Training or coaching?

The next stage is to identify which areas are suitable for off-the-job training and which are suitable for coaching on the job.

Staff member	*Areas for development*	*Training*	*Coaching*
1.			
2.			
3.			

Implementing the development

The next step is to implement the development you have identified as necessary in the way you have chosen. This will involve a discussion with each person to discuss development needs and to arrive at a joint agreement about the way forward. At this stage you need to take account of any barriers to effective development.

For example, how is training viewed in your section? Is it viewed as a punishment or a reward, or are people sent on training courses because it is their turn?

Preparing and debriefing the individual

If training has been agreed, the final stage is to prepare the individual for it. You as a manager have a very important part to play in ensuring that training is effective. After the training has taken place you also need to debrief the individual and discuss ways of putting into practice the skills and knowledge he or she has acquired.

If you have decided on coaching as a way to develop members of staff, you now need to plan and implement the coaching programme.

Exercise 9.4 Developing fit teams: How easy will it be?

To make the best use of a team-building activity the group needs to be ready for it. This exercise will help you assess whether the groups in your organization are ready for team building. It will also provide information which will help you plan a strategy for improving group working. Consider each team with which you are connected, and answer the following questions:

yes/no

1. Does the group have a task which requires that it works together to achieve objectives?
2. Is the group willing to devote time to improving its effectiveness as a group?
3. Does the formal leader want to develop the team?
4. Do the members of the group want to develop their effectiveness as a group?
5. Does the team have regular meetings?
6. Is the group's task important to the organization as a whole?
7. Do top management support a team style of management?

Yes answers to these questions are an indication that the group is a suitable one for a team-development exercise. If the team you are considering does not fulfil the necessary criteria, you will need to prepare the ground before a specific team-development activity takes place.

Are there any steps you need to take to prepare the ground for team developments?

The next step is deciding whether or not to use an outsider — a consultant who will facilitate the development of the team. The team should start the development process by reviewing how they currently work and what their concerns are. The areas for concern and development can then be identified and worked on.

Exercise 9.5 The unfit organization: How to avoid it

In this exercise we are asking you to consider whether your organization is an unfit and stressful place to work by designing an organization that actually works to create stress. By designing such an organization in your imagination you can compare an extreme model with the real organization in which you work. It is easier to envisage this extreme than an organization completely without stress. It provides a basis for assessing and improving your own organization.

Imagine the most unfit organization you can think of. Consider as many aspects of the organization as you can; the headings below will guide your thinking.

Organizational structure

Consider the design of the unfit organization. How is the work divided? What is the hierarchical arrangement? How is the work integrated?

Organizational systems

Consider the systems which operate in the unfit organization. What personnel systems does it have? What systems for financial control?

Organization culture

Consider the culture of the unfit organization. What are they key values held? What are the core beliefs?

Physical environment

Consider the physical environment of the unfit organization. What is the physical layout of the organization? What are the physical conditions of work?

Job design

Consider the jobs in the unfit organization. What are they? Are job descriptions clear? Is the work routine?

Other aspects

Consider any other aspects you can think of which would make for an unfit organization.

Your organization

Now consider your organization in the light of your description of an unfit organization. Does your organization have any unfit aspects? List them below.

Finally, consider what steps could be taken to overcome the unfit aspects of your organization and plan a strategy for change. Consider each aspect in turn.

Unfit aspect	*Desired state*	*Steps to bring about change*
1.		
2.		
3.		
4.		

Appendix 1. Organizational stress management: The way ahead

Organizations need not rely on a few, motivated managers to cope with pressure and survive. Many organizations are setting up stress-management programmes to make a major impact on the whole organization. Such programmes ensure that individuals learn to manage pressure and that managers are proactive in making the organization fit and able to cope. Most importantly, they ensure a climate in which stress is seen as an important management concern. Programmes can involve seminars and training programmes, team workshops, the provision of a professional source of individual counselling, and opportunities for people to learn and use healthy life habits. Organizations succeed through the people they employ, and success is enhanced when they find ways of making pressure work for, not against their staff.

When an organization develops its staff and its work groups and devotes attention to the design of the organization as a whole it will increase its fitness and adaptability. It will do more than that, however, for while an organization needs to be flexible when adapting to change, a fit organization not only reacts to events but becomes proactive and creates changes in the world outside. A successful organization is more than fit; it becomes a market leader and world beater.

Just as each manager needs to maintain his or her optimum pressure level to deal with his or her own stress, so an organization needs to maintain its pressure at the optimum level. Managers who are not stressed have energy for managing staff effectively. Organizations which are not stressed can turn their attention to the outside world.

The key to managing pressure is creating and using a survival guide. There is no single device which will ensure survival, but if you reduce unnecessary pressure, equip yourself with personal and managerial skills and take time to become personally and organizationally fitter and more resilient, you will not only survive as a manager but succeed.

Appendix 2. Further Reading

If you are interested in exploring the area of stress management further, these are some of the books which we have found helpful and which we recommend.

Adler, Richard *Beating Your Heart,* Corgi, London, 1985.

Albrecht, Karl, *Stress and the Manager,* Prentice-Hall, Englewood Cliffs, NJ, 1979.

Back, Kate and Ken, *Assertiveness at work,* McGraw-Hill, Maidenhead, 1982.

Benson, Herbert, *The Relaxation Response,* Collins, Fount paperbacks, London, 1975.

Egan, Gerard, *The Skilled Helper,* Brooks/Cole, Monterey, California, 1981.

Hastings, C., P. Bixby and R. Chaudhry-Lawton, *The Superteam Solution,* Gower, Aldershot, 1986.

James, Muriel and Dorothy Jongeward, *Born to Win,* Addison-Wesley, Reading, Mass., 1971.

Klein, Mavis, *Lives People Live,* John Wiley, Chichester, 1980.

Livingstone-Booth, Audrey, *Stressmanship,* Severn House, London, 1985.

Madders, Jane, *Stress and Relaxation,* Martin Dunitz, London, 1979.

Mintzburg, Henry, *Structure in Fives: Designing Effective Organisations,* Prentice-Hall, New Jersey, 1983.

Megginson, David, and Tom Boydell, *A Manager's Guide to Coaching,* BACIE, London, 1979.

Quick, James C. and Jonathan D., *Organisational Stress and Preventive Management,* McGraw-Hill, New York, 1984.

Selye, Hans, *The Stress of Life,* McGraw-Hill, New York, 1978.

Smith, Manual J., *When I Say No, I Feel Guilty,* Bantam, New York, 1975.

Toffler, Alvin, *Future Shock,* Pan Books, London, 1970.

Watts, A.G. (ed.), *Counselling at Work,* Bedford Square Press, London, 1977.

Woodcock, Mike, and Dave Francis, *Organisation Development through Teambuilding,* Gower, Aldershot, 1981.

Index